T0081002

Presented to:

....

From:

....

Date:

....

BOOKS BY GARY THOMAS

Authentic Faith

Cherish

Devotions for a Sacred Marriage

Devotions for Sacred Parenting

Every Body Matters

The Glorious Pursuit

Holy Available

A Lifelong Love

Loving Him Well

Preparing Your Heart for Marriage

Pure Pleasure

Sacred Influence

Sacred Marriage

Sacred Parenting

Sacred Pathways

The Sacred Search

Thirsting for God

PREPARING
Your
HEART
for
MARRIAGE

Devotions for
Engaged Couples

PREPARING
Your
HEART
for
MARRIAGE

Devotions for
Engaged Couples

GARY THOMAS

ZONDERVAN®
.com

ZONDERVAN
Preparing Your Heart for Marriage

Copyright © 2018 by Gary L. Thomas

Published in Grand Rapids, Michigan, by Zondervan. Zondervan is a registered trademark of The Zondervan Corporation, L.L.C., a wholly owned subsidiary of HarperCollins Christian Publishing, Inc.

Requests for information should be addressed to customercare@harpercollins.com.

ISBN 978-0-310-45203-4 (audiobook)
ISBN 978-0-310-34596-1 (HC)

Published in association with Yates & Yates, LLP, Attorneys and Counselors, Orange, California.

All Scripture quotations, unless otherwise indicated, are taken from *The Holy Bible, New International Version*, NIV. Copyright © 1973, 1978, 1984, 2011 by Biblica, Inc. Used by permission of Zondervan. All rights reserved worldwide. www.zondervan.com. The "NIV" and "New International Version" are trademarks registered in the United States Patent and Trademark Office by Biblica, Inc.

Scripture quotations marked BSB are taken from the Holy Bible, Berean Study Bible (BSB) © 2016 by Bible Hub. Used by permission. All rights reserved worldwide.

Scripture quotations marked ESV are taken from the ESV Bible (The Holy Bible, English Standard Version). Copyright © 2001 by Crossway, a publishing ministry of Good News Publishers. Used by permission. All rights reserved.

Scripture quotations marked NLT are taken from the Holy Bible, New Living Translation, copyright © 1996, 2004, 2015 by Tyndale House Foundation. Used by permission of Tyndale House Ministries, Carol Stream, Illinois 60188. All rights reserved.

Scripture quotations marked NRSV are taken from the New Revised Standard Version Bible. Copyright © 1989 National Council of the Churches of Christ in the United States of America. Used by permission. All rights reserved worldwide.

Any Internet addresses (websites, blogs, etc.) and telephone numbers in this book are offered as a resource. They are not intended in any way to be or imply an endorsement by Zondervan, nor does Zondervan vouch for the content of these sites and numbers for the life of this book.

All rights reserved. No part of this publication may be reproduced, stored in a retrieval system, or transmitted in any form or by any means—electronic, mechanical, photocopy, recording, or any other—except for brief quotations in printed reviews, without the prior permission of the publisher.

Cover design: Bruce DeRoos
Interior design: Kristy Edwards
Author Photo: Jaclyn Boutwell

Printed in Malaysia

24 25 26 27 28 29 30 / OFF / 14 13 12 11 10 9 8 7 6 5

Lisa and I dedicate this book to two dear friends who are also two champions of marriage: Doug and Julie Macrae. They have selflessly blessed our own marriage, and have worked faithfully to bless the marriages of many others.

CONTENTS

CONGRATULATIONS!

∞

He who finds a wife finds what is good
and receives favor from the LORD.

PROVERBS 18:22

As a pastor I have officiated at many weddings, but the ceremonies never become old to me. They are charged with spiritual power and the amazing miracle—I don't use that word lightly—of God turning two people into one. From the wedding day forward, the person with whom you are going through this devotional will always be a part of you in a unique way.

So, allow me to congratulate you on this momentous choice to get married. Engagement is bursting with promise, hopes, joys, and anticipations of all kinds. It can also be one of the busiest times of your life. For some, planning a wedding, with all the decisions involved, can feel more arduous than launching a business, starting a church, or certainly, writing a book. Kudos to you two for wanting to make spiritual preparation a part of this special, albeit busy, season.

Amid the busyness, this devotional is designed to help you think through the spiritual priorities and challenges that lie ahead in order to grow an outstanding marriage. It is not designed for those who need help evaluating each other and are still asking the question, should we get married? For couples in that season, I'd recommend my book *The Sacred Search* (Colorado Springs: David C. Cook, 2013). This volume is to help those who have already made the decision to get married and want to start growing together right away, as well as prepare, spiritually speaking, for a very special day and the life beyond it.

The first half will deal with various issues that are essential to know going into marriage. A successful marriage is about who you are as much as it is about what you do, so these devotions are designed to help you grow in the Lord as you grow closer to each other. The second half focuses exclusively on the traditional statement of intent and the traditional wedding vows. Though you may not choose to use this language in your ceremony, there is a richness to the time-honored truth represented by these promises. Talking about these truths, praying over them, and discussing the implications together will make your wedding ceremony all the more special and meaningful. You'll be familiar with every word you promise, making you more present for the ceremony and more engaged in the miracle taking place: two people becoming one.

Choosing to make spiritual preparation a part of your premarital efforts is a wise thing to do. I pray God will use each devotion to bless you spiritually and relationally as you seek to grow ever closer to Christ and closer to each other.

PART 1

GOD'S PLAN FOR MARRIAGE

———— ∞∞ ————

Though I'm sure you're thrilled with each other, the reality is that no one person is spiritually complete and ready for marriage, "finished" to the extent that he or she doesn't need to grow any more. These devotions are designed to help you search your heart so that you can give the very best you—and a progressively maturing you—to your future spouse.

Twenty years of marriage ministry and more than thirty years of being married myself have convinced me that the closer you draw to Christ, the closer you can draw to each other. And the holier you become, reflecting the virtues and characteristics of Christ, the happier you'll become in your marriage.

1

CELEBRATING THE
JOYS OF MARRIAGE

Many waters cannot quench love;
rivers cannot sweep it away.
If one were to give
all the wealth of one's house for love,
it would be utterly scorned.

SONG OF SONGS 8:7

I thought I was one of the world's biggest fans of marriage, until I asked a question on Facebook ("What do you love most about marriage?") and found out there are a ton of marriage fans out there! Perhaps it'll encourage you to hear so many positive reports about what married people love about being married as you prepare to become married.

In *Sacred Marriage* I wrote:

I love marriage, and I love my marriage. I love the fun parts, the easy parts, and the pleasurable parts, but also the difficult parts— the parts that frustrate me but help me understand myself and my spouse on a deeper level; the parts that are painful but that crucify the aspects of me that I hate; the parts that force me to my knees and teach me that I need to learn to love with God's love instead of just trying harder. Marriage has led me to deeper levels of understanding, more pronounced worship, and a sense of fellowship that I never knew existed.[1]

Sacred Marriage admits how difficult marriage can be, but also points out that when it is good, it can be *very* good. As Jillian responded on Facebook, "Marriage is hard . . . especially when you're acting selfish . . . but it's also an absolute blast!"

So many singles who have witnessed some truly awful marriages ask me, "Is marriage worth the risk?" Accordingly, I asked married couples on my Facebook pages to brag about the benefits of marriage. When asked what they loved *most* about marriage, the most common answer was "friendship, companionship, and sharing life together." Ecclesiastes 4:9–12 captures this gift of marriage:

Two people are better off than one, for they can help each other succeed. If one person falls, the other can reach out and help. But someone who falls alone is in real trouble. Likewise, two people lying close together can keep each other warm. But how can one be warm alone? A person standing alone can be attacked and defeated, but two can stand back-to-back and conquer. (NLT)

Second, married couples talked about the spiritual benefit of pursuing God together. You don't just gain a husband or wife when you get married; you live with a brother or sister in Christ. You will never experience such a level of accountability and the possibility of encouragement and inspiration with anyone else quite like you can with your spouse. This reminds me of Hebrews 3:13–14: "But encourage one another daily, as long as it is called 'Today,' so that none of you may be hardened by sin's deceitfulness. We have come to share in Christ."

> You don't just gain a husband or wife when you get married; you live with a brother or sister in Christ.

Shelly wrote this about the spiritual benefits of her marriage:

[My marriage] has caused me to grow closer to God than I ever imagined possible and strengthened that relationship first, so that I can see my husband, my best friend with more of His eyes and consequently love my husband in a deeper, more meaningful way that is connected to Christ. Without my marriage, my relationship with God and others would be less complete.

Third, couples praised the wonder of sexual intimacy within

marriage, when there is an amazing spiritual bond, relational bond, and incredible physical sensations, not to mention the exhilarating feelings of closeness afterwards. Few highs in life will ever come close to sexual intimacy in marriage. Song of Songs 5:1 exalts,

> *I came to my garden, my sister, my bride,*
> *I gathered my myrrh with my spice,*
> *I ate my honeycomb with my honey,*
> *I drank my wine with my milk.*
> *Eat, friends, drink,*
> *and be drunk with love!* (ESV)

Having each other's back was another benefit of marriage named by our Facebook respondents. I love the way Lindsey captured her marriage with Steve: "Knowing that no matter what the world, the family, friends, or even the church tosses at me—my man always has my back and loves me even when I am wrong. It's the peace of knowing my heart is in his hand."

Reed said something similar from a man's perspective when he praised "the warm embrace and kindness of my wife when I come home after the world has beat on me all day long, and her heart of defense for me and our marriage as a team and unit."

Other benefits of marriage people identified included these:

- knowing to whom your first call will be (for good news or bad)
- facing sickness and life disappointments (unemployment, the death of loved ones, etc.) together
- someone to celebrate with

- a treasure trove of inside jokes
- quiet evenings or mornings where you're doing nothing, but you're doing nothing *together*
- growing old together
- sharing parenting duties together

Alison added, "Being each other's sounding board! Offering each other an ear when one needs to vent or one wants to share ideas or ask questions! I love it!" And Reno wrote about "the sharing of life experiences . . . the look across a crowded room that says, 'Let's go home.'"

I personally love having someone to bless, and several others said the same thing. The Bible calls us to be devoted to good works (Titus 3:8, 14 ESV), and it's a great joy to do things for your spouse that make her or his life easier or more pleasant. If you live a life of worship and walk in grace, you'll feel *compelled* to love and serve others. God's Holy Spirit orients you toward a life of blessing, and marriage provides the most immediate context in which to live that out.

Alison's words capture the wonder of marriage as well as anyone's could. In fact, her words are so beautiful and true to life, let's end this devotion with her reflections:

I realized this summer what I love most. I have gone on a few trips to visit family with just my kids. Greg has stayed behind to work. After a few days I was ready to go home. I missed being home. This summer our family of five took an almost two-week road trip and there wasn't one second I wanted to go home. I looked at Greg one evening and told him he was my *home*. Wherever he is, I am home. Thinking about what home represents summarizes marriage to me—so much security, love, family time, rest, quiet times with Jesus, safety in storms of life; that is my husband and my favorite part of marriage.

Marriage is a great way to live!

———— ⬭ ————

Heavenly Father, thank you so, so much for helping us find each other and for creating the relationship of marriage, which has the potential to bless us in so many ways. We recognize marriage to be a good gift, given by you, and we celebrate you for it. In Jesus' name, amen.

———— ⬭ ————

Questions for Reflection

✳ Describe the positive qualities of marriages you've witnessed; what did/do you like about these couples' relationships? What inspires you about the way they love each other?

✳ What two or three things are you most looking forward to about marriage?

2

GOD'S INVENTION

That is why a man leaves his father
and mother and is united to his wife,
and they become one flesh.

GENESIS 2:24

James Naismith invented basketball.

A Yale medical student named Walter Camp is most responsible for the game Americans now call football.

The origins of baseball are a little more dubious. Traditionally, Abner Doubleday was given the honors, but historians now believe the game largely evolved, slowly and methodically, from a number of different sources.

The origin of marriage, however, is much clearer. We know exactly when it was created and by whom: at the beginning of human existence, marriage was created by God. God gave the first woman to the first man and told both of them that this would be their primary relationship: "That is why a man leaves his father and mother and is united to his wife, and they become one flesh" (Genesis 2:24).

Before there was any government; before there was a single church; before there was any business or a sports team of any kind, there was *marriage*.

You are signing up for something God designed and that has been in existence since the very beginning.

Marriage didn't evolve from human ingenuity. It wasn't one of several options tried through the centuries until the consensus came down that the joining of one man and one woman for life is the best way to organize society. According to Scripture, there was never a time when more than one human existed and marriage didn't. God thought up marriage, and most of us go along with him.

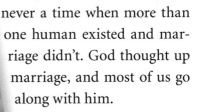

Since we didn't invent marriage, we don't get to set the rules. In a very real sense, once we commit to marriage, we must learn to *receive* marriage as God designed it. I can't overstate how helpful this surrender to marriage as God designed it can be for you in the coming years.

Being married has brought me tremendous joy, but marriage isn't always easy or pleasant. Plus, there are many voices that tear down the notion of marriage, which might, if we listen, make us feel less enthusiastic about our own marriage or the wisdom of choosing to get married. Reminding yourself that "this whole marriage thing" is God's idea will help keep you going when times get tough.

> Reminding yourself that "this whole marriage thing" is God's idea will help keep you going when times get tough.

Hundreds of years ago, Martin Luther warned young men about popular voices that talk negatively about marriage.

In Luther's mind, understanding the true nobility of marriage as God designed it is essential for us to experience the full joy of marriage. In his essay "The Estate of Marriage," he explained why it's not enough to simply *be* married. We should recognize the "estate of marriage," and by that he meant accepting that God created the concept of marriage and wants most of us to submit to it.

To recognize the estate of marriage is something quite different from merely being married. He who is married but does not recognize the estate of marriage cannot continue in wedlock without bitterness, drudgery, and anguish; he will inevitably complain . . . Now the ones who recognize the estate of marriage are those who firmly believe that God himself instituted it, brought husband and wife together, and ordained that they should beget children and care for them. For this they have God's word [Genesis 1:28], and they can be certain that he does not lie. They can therefore also be certain that the estate of marriage and everything that goes with it in the way of conduct, works, and suffering is pleasing to God. Now tell me, how can the heart have greater good, joy, and delight than in God, when one is certain that his estate, conduct, and work is pleasing to God?[1]

It is this assurance that God has called us into marriage that will most help us when marriage becomes a struggle. Luther urged us to remember that *even the most difficult aspects of wedlock* bring joy when we see that they are part of God's plan for us. In Luther's view, because God has created marriage, we, his children and followers, should embrace all aspects of it—even the tough parts—because we know it is his will and his design to grow us and to build society.

Luther summed it up this way:

I say these things in order that we may learn how honorable a thing it is to live in that estate which God has ordained. In it we find God's word and good pleasure, by which all the works, conduct, and sufferings of that estate become holy, godly, and precious so that Solomon even congratulates such a man and says in Proverbs 5 [:18], "Rejoice in the wife of your youth," and again in Ecclesiastes 11 [9:9], "Enjoy life with the wife whom you love all the days of your vain life." Solomon . . . is . . . offering godly comfort to those who find much drudgery in married life.[2]

On your wedding day, it is the pastor's job to remind you that God is the One who designed and created marriage as a lifelong institution between one man and one woman. The fact that God created and called us into marriage makes this estate a holy one, a right one, and a spiritually healthy one. Therefore, marriage—with all its joys and all its trials, all its comforts and all its suffering, all its happiness and all its pain—is good.

Will you join hands with your beloved and acknowledge that marriage is God's idea and that in addition to making a commitment to each other, you're planning to surrender to his design and will for the rest of your life?

———⧜———

Heavenly Father, we know from your Word that you are a kind and generous God. When you call us to join hands in marriage and raise kids, you do so knowing that it won't always be easy for us, but even the difficult seasons have purpose and meaning. We recognize marriage is something you created and that the idea of making vows to each other is surrendering to your plan for our lives. Help us remember the day we utter these vows that we're making as not just to each other, but before you. In Jesus' name, amen.

Questions for Reflection

✱ What do you think the difference is between a marriage that is viewed as a legal contract and one that is entered into as a divinely designed covenant?

✱ As your wedding day draws near, what is a healthy way to respond when people say things like, "About to get the old ball and chain, huh?" "Enjoy your freedom while you can!" "Why would you ever want to give up your singleness?" Now that you understand marriage as an "estate" from God, what's the best way to accept this for yourself and communicate it to others when they talk it down?

3

YOU'RE GOING ON A JOURNEY

*Encourage one another and build each
other up, just as in fact you are doing.*

1 THESSALONIANS 5:11

One of the most common questions I get about my book for singles, *The Sacred Search*, which gives a lot of advice about what to look for and what to avoid when choosing someone to marry, is, "What if I can't find a person like the one you describe?"

Singles who ask this question reveal a fundamental misunderstanding of marriage. Marriage is a *journey*, not a *destination*. To explain what that means, as well as the difference that makes, let me ask you a couple of questions:

What did you imagine your future spouse would be like?

How close is that "imaginary" spouse to your fiancé/fiancée?

In his book *Letters to Malcolm, Chiefly on Prayer*, C. S. Lewis told a friend, "You and I have both known happy marriage. But how different our wives were from the imaginary mistresses of our adolescent dreams! So much less exquisitely adapted to all our wishes; and for that very reason (among others) so incomparably better."[1]

The real will never equate to the imaginary; we naturally assume that means the real will never live up to the imaginary. But Lewis suggests (and he's correct) that though the real won't seem to be as good a fit in theory, the real will actually be much better than the imaginary.

How is this so?

It's the nature of fulfillment in a fallen world. When we "dream" of a spouse, we don't dream of things to overcome; we dream of battles already won. We dream of the victory, not the fight; the ecstasy, not the moments of doubt. We dream of the moments of tenderness, not the storms of misunderstanding. We dream of intimacy, not lonely nights of distance. But it's the battles, the fights, the doubts and the storms that make up so much of what marriage actually is; it's having to overcome those challenges that makes us grow; and the presence of those challenges makes overcoming them all the sweeter, richer, purer, and ultimately more fulfilling.

That's why the question, "Where do I find someone like this to marry?" fails to take into account that marriage is a *journey*, not a *destination.* It's a journey toward each other, toward God, toward growth, toward maturity, perhaps toward children, eventually, toward heaven. *Enjoy the journey*; don't let it be eclipsed because you haven't yet arrived at the destination. Overcoming obstacles is part of every "championship season."

Writing as a man who is now in his thirty-third year of marriage, I can honestly say that marriage has never been sweeter. My wife and I had some difficult seasons early on, but there are moments now, just going on a bike ride or seeing the sun catch her smile just right, that make me swoon like a teenager. She is the delight of my life. But it was a journey to get to this place. Marriage has brought me many of my happiest moments in life, but it has not been one solid state of always being happy, or even being increasingly happy. You might, along the way, have to walk through a few dark valleys that feel like a setback.

Some of you, with high expectations, hope to inherit heaven immediately by making a wise marital choice. But be forewarned: the only way to get to heaven is to die, not to get married. Here on earth, we travel toward heaven, and I've found, as many have, that my preference is to travel with a lifelong companion, even one who is not perfect.

> The joy of marriage isn't that there are no more battles; it's that you never have to face a battle alone.

If you ask your future spouse to be your destination—the one who completes you, makes everything better, and leaves you always feeling completely satisfied (which is what we thought our imaginary spouse would do and be), you will bury him or her with your expectations and resent it when your spouse's ill health inconveniences you. You're not choosing a destination; you're choosing a traveling partner, someone which

whom you can grow. The joy of marriage isn't that there are no more battles; it's that you never have to face a battle alone.

You'll discover soon after you are married that one of the reasons "fantasy" spouses don't exist in real life is because just about every relational strength comes with a corresponding weakness—the patient man may be, at times, a little too passive. The fun woman may, at times, be a little too irresponsible. The pious man may, at times, seem to hold you accountable just when you wish he wouldn't. The organized woman may feel controlling. These are the layers of relationship, and they're what makes growth possible.

That is why you need to die to the fantasy of arriving in order to begin the journey of becoming. Until you desire the real more than you do the phantom, you're not ready to be married.

Remember: you're accepting your spouse's weaknesses as you receive his or her strengths. That's the only attitude that will help you fulfill the call to "encourage one another and build each other up" (1 Thess. 5:11). There would be no need to encourage and build up your spouse unless your spouse occasionally breaks down. Marriage is often about helping each other get back up even more than it is about entering an early paradise.

Heavenly Father, help me to accept my future spouse as a traveling partner as we journey toward your will for our lives. I know we will struggle at times; I realize we will frustrate each other; I'm sure the day will come when marriage will feel like a lot of hard work. Help us to embrace these moments as part of the purpose of marriage—to encourage and build each other up as often as life seems to break us down.

Questions for Reflection

※ Spend some time talking with each other about what you imagined your future spouse would be like when you were younger. In what ways does your current fiancé/fiancée resemble this imaginary spouse? In what ways might he or she differ?

※ Are you the kind of person who just expects/ wants marriage to be easy? Do you think you're prepared for the spiritual challenge of encouraging each other and building each other back up when you become emotionally discouraged or physically sick?

※ Why is it important to view marriage as a journey rather than a destination?

4

A NEW DIMENSION

∞

*Accept one another, then, just
as Christ accepted you, in order
to bring praise to God.*

ROMANS 15:7

Dating and/or living together are as far from marriage as Singapore is from Seattle. Marriage requires making a conscious mental and heart shift to enter into what is an entirely new dimension of relationship.

In dating, there is a natural, healthy period of evaluation. As a couple, you're getting to know each other to determine if this is a relationship that will work:

Is this person trustworthy?

Is his faith real?

Is she responsible?

Would he make a good parent?

Is she someone I'd like to spend every day with for the rest of my life?

These are healthy, even necessary questions. And to

some extent, until you put a ring on each other's finger and say, "I do," such questions never fully stop. But once the bride is kissed, the rice is thrown, and the marriage is consummated, *everything changes*. Evaluations must cease. You will discover things about each other that you missed. You will learn new things that may not be pleasing and that may, in fact, be a bit scary.* But now the question isn't whether to run the race but how to keep running the race.

The Comrades Marathon is a world-famous, fifty-six-mile race in South Africa. Every year, the course is reversed. One year is called the "up" year and one year is called the "down" year, though both years are hilly, and both directions bring a different kind of pain. You can choose which year you want to run. You get the same medal, and the same amount of time (twelve hours) to finish the race. There's no shame in choosing any one particular course. But once the gun goes off, you have to finish the race you've chosen.

Your wedding day is like that. When the pastor says, "I now pronounce you husband and wife," that's your "starting gun." You've

---

* By using the word "scary" here, I want to make it clear I am *not* referring to ever tolerating domestic violence. "Accepting each other" does *not* mean accepting abuse.

chosen your course, so to speak, by choosing the person you've agreed to marry. That choice will involve certain challenges, as no one is really all that easy to love. Every person requires some accommodation. But keep reminding yourself: "This is the course I've chosen, and it's too late to reevaluate now. At this point, I need to focus on running."

Are you ready, spiritually, to accept your future spouse, just as he or she is? You know he or she is not perfect, so you will have to learn to live with the imperfections. You can't marry a life-of-the-party extrovert and then complain that he tends to be loud at social gatherings. You can't marry a somewhat shy introvert and be frustrated that she doesn't enjoy frequent and long parties. Once your spouse-to-be is yours, you "own" his or her issues and will live with those issues and have to accept them as your new reality.

Once the wedding is over, reevaluating a marital choice becomes a trap, as it will simply take needed energy away from improving the marriage. That's why thoughtful and wise evaluation leading to acceptance *before the marriage* is so important. Evaluating (including seeking wise advice and counsel) is essential before the wedding, but after the wedding day it can become poisonous.

> **Evaluating is essential before the wedding, but after the wedding day it can become poisonous.**

One thing I like to do when I counsel a premarital couple is have each identify the other's three greatest weaknesses. If they can't think of any weaknesses, they don't know each other well enough to be married, as everyone has at least three. The purpose is to get them to this place of spiritual acceptance. They're admitting that they know this is what they are choosing, so when a weakness creeps

up after marriage, they can accept their choice rather than reevaluate it.

Putting a ring on the finger of a chronically late person won't make him suddenly start showing up on time just because he is married to you. Exchanging vows with an addict won't cure her addiction—it just weds you to her vulnerability for the rest of your life together. A homebody marrying a party-hearty social butterfly won't make the social butterfly happy to stay home more often than not.

People usually don't change, so your heart must. You must learn to think, *This is the person I've chosen. How can I build the best life possible with him [her], just as he [she] is?*

Another way to look at this is as if you're building a new house, and on the day of your wedding, all of the materials are delivered. You can't go back to the store to get new materials. You have to build the best house you can with what is already on the lot. If you have bricks, you can build a brick house. If not, you're going to have to be content with wood. Every moment spent wishing you had chosen to have bricks delivered is wasted time and energy. Instead, you should put all your energy into building the most beautiful and functional house possible with the materials that you have on hand.

———————— ∞ ————————

Father, now that I have found someone to marry, help me move from evaluation to appreciation, from critique to encouragement. Let me bury any thought of "what if . . ." or "if only . . ." and instead focus on how to make the best of this union. In Jesus' name, amen.

Questions for Reflection

✳ Write down your future spouse's three biggest weaknesses. Will you accept these weaknesses and pledge to honor, support, and appreciate your spouse from here on out?

✳ Are you at the place where you can unequivocally state that you have made your choice, and now evaluation is no longer appropriate? If so, think up a mental strategy to deal with evaluative-type questions. How can you catch yourself ruminating on "if only"-type thoughts? With what will you replace them?

✳ Imagine living under the perpetual stare of being evaluated and potentially cut from a sports team or job. If you don't produce on any given day, your business or team can let you go. Now imagine the security of having a lifetime contract that can't be broken—the peace, the security, the sense of well-being. Will you give that lifetime contract to your future spouse? How will your words and actions help reinforce the security of that contract?

5

MAKE MY DREAMS
COME TRUE

⚬⚬⚬⚬

Let each of you look out not only for his own
interests, but also for the interests of others.

PHILIPPIANS 2:4

Way, way, *way* back in 1981—before my wife and I were even dating, much less married—a very popular song by a very popular duo (Hall and Oates) rocketed up the charts: "You Make My Dreams Come True."

The song title captures the reality many of us search for: someone to "make my dreams come true." It may be the dream of a perfect wedding day. It may be the dream of a perfect home, a perfect life, a perfect companion. *Whatever my dreams may be*, you think, *please, please, please make them come true.*

Dreams of perfection can cause a lot of stress, and some dreams need to be discarded when we compare them to God's call on our lives. But one of the many joys of marriage is gaining an advocate for each other's dreams. Your dreams become my dreams. My dreams become your dreams. Philippians 2:4 tells us, "Each of you should look not only to your own interests, but also to the interests of others" (BSB).

The day you get married, you sign up to become an advocate for your spouse's dreams. Your attitude should be "How can I make *your* dreams come true?"

If marriage is about signing up to help make each other's dreams come true, it's wise to consider whether you are reasonably able to do that. Some dreams are incompatible.

> The day you get married, you sign up to become an advocate for your spouse's dreams.

I've counseled some couples where the wife has always wanted to stay home with the kids when they are young. That's something that in today's economy takes a lot of planning. But future husband, if this is what your wife wants, there will always be a bit of frustration she must fight against if you don't make an earnest effort to help her achieve that dream.

Other wives may want to and expect to have their spouses' support to pursue their vocations even while raising kids. Or perhaps the husband wants to stay home. Keep in mind, however, that you *both* may have to sacrifice when you consider what is best not just for each other, but for your kids.

I've seen wives accept a lower standard of living and be the only ones bringing home any significant income while their husbands

pursued a writing or pho-
tography career. Some
husbands have taken two
jobs so their wives can
complete an advanced
degree. Some have accepted
living in a town or city that
isn't all that exciting to them
because they know it's where
their spouses really want to
live or where their spouses'
extended family lives.

Spend some time talking
about your dreams in every area
of life. Make this exciting. What
have you always wanted to do, but
weren't sure you had it in you to do it? Can your spouse help resurrect
that dream and make it happen? After sharing your dreams, spend a
little time making sure your dreams are compatible. If getting married is about saying, "I want to help make your dreams come true,"
ask yourself: "Am I willing to spend a significant portion of my life,
my resources, and my time helping my spouse achieve this particular
dream?"

∞

*Heavenly Father, we realize that marriage isn't just
about living in the same house. It's about building a life
together, and part of life is pursuing dreams. Help us*

understand the dreams that best reflect who you made us to be and that align with your purposes for us. Give us unselfish hearts so that we can truly care about each other's dreams as much as we care about our own. In Jesus' name, amen.

Questions for Reflection

✻ Share two or three lifelong dreams with each other—the kind of dreams that you will be truly disappointed about if they don't come true sometime in your lifetime.

✻ How will you prioritize these dreams? Whose will come first? Why?

✻ Take some steps to start working toward those dreams *today.* Marriage is more meaningful when you "hit the ground running"— when you have something pulling the two of you forward and together before you even get married.

6

THE MOST IMPORTANT THINGS

❀

"Seek first the kingdom of God and
his righteousness, and all these things
will be added to you [as well]."

MATTHEW 6:33 (ESV)

O ne of the most important skills you need in order to excel in marriage is rarely talked about, but it's essential: *focus.*

A great marriage is all about maintaining the right focus on the most important things.

One of the first things I go over with engaged couples is to ask them to make a commitment that they will not discuss the wedding ceremony at least three days out of seven. It is so easy to let a thirty- to

sixty-minute ceremony become your focus for the next nine months, but you should be preparing for life more than you should be preparing for a party.

Otherwise, here's what you can expect: you spend your dates and downtime talking about the flowers, the venue, the guest list, the tux, the songs, the wedding party, the reception, the food, the music, and on and on. Obsessive talk creates an obsessive focus, which changes the character of your relationship to anticipation instead of relation. As the wedding day draws near, you keep saying to each other, "Can you believe it's almost here?" and you worry about the details and talk about who can't make it, and so on.

The ceremony happens—it's almost over before you know it—and you embark on your honeymoon. You spend two days reliving the ceremony (who was there, who wasn't, what went right, what was funny, could you believe he said that, or that she did that?), and by about the third day of the honeymoon, the ceremony is talked out.

What your relationship has been built on for months is over.

What do you talk about now?

It's not just about conversation—it's about adrenaline. When you invest too much in a party and the party is now past, there's a natural letdown. You've invested so much in this day, looked forward to this day, set your hopes on this day, and now that it's over, how can you not feel a little depressed?

Do you really want to feel depressed on your honeymoon?

How do you counter this?

You focus. You guard your heart so that what you're living for is still in front of you. The most wonderful feeling in the world is to be intoxicatingly in love with your new spouse, enjoying your time together, *but eager to get back to life.* Then it's not about what's past, but about what's ahead.

You get to this blessed place by realizing that a marriage matters far more than a ceremony, that the wedding is just the first day of hopefully tens of thousands of days.

If you spend your engaged months seeking first God's kingdom (looking to reach out to others, thinking about others, serving others, on his behalf) and his righteousness (growing in grace, kindness, surrender, humility), then you are spiritually preparing yourself for a spectacular marriage.

The problem with taking a vacation from Matthew 6:33—even to plan something so life changing as a wedding ceremony—is that it sets you up to be selfish, and selfishness destroys more marriages than just about anything else.

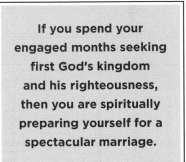

If you spend your engaged months seeking first God's kingdom and his righteousness, then you are spiritually preparing yourself for a spectacular marriage.

You worry about impressing people with the cake more than about impressing them with God's grace. You worry about how you'll look in a dress or a tux more than whether your attitude reflects the kindness and patience of Christ. And if you do that for six months or nine months or a year, it turns you into the kind of person who is self-obsessed.

A self-obsessed person doesn't do so well in marriage.

In other words, this waiting and preparation for marriage will shape you into the kind of person who excels in marriage, or the kind of person who sabotages his or her marriage.

If you can't focus on God's kingdom and righteousness now, and you let a wedding ceremony become your focus, then after marriage, you'll slip into focusing on buying and setting up your house and other such matters. It never ends. There's always something that feels more pressing than seeking first God's kingdom and righteousness.

It takes a certain spiritual maturity to be able to set aside something really exciting and discipline yourself to choose to focus on something eternal. But that's the obedient life in summary. Not that the eternal isn't exciting—it is! But our hearts tend to follow our minds. If you set your mind to always think about a ceremony, you squeeze out thinking about anything else, and thus your heart drifts from everything else.

The ceremony should serve your marriage, not sabotage it. Set aside at least three days a week where you will not discuss wedding details. Maybe you'll lead or participate in a small group, find a creative way to serve others, just sit and listen to a grandparent, meet with another couple that's struggling, or go out and have a very fun time together.

Learn the secret of focus, and you'll plant the seeds for an intimate, fulfilling, and lifelong love.

Heavenly Father, help us learn to focus on your kingdom—doing your work, serving others, reaching out—and growing in righteousness over the coming months. Lead us to think more about whether we are reflecting Christ than whether we can impress others with the ceremony. Reveal to us things to do together; point out personal areas where we need to grow. Let this ceremony remind us to choose the best things first rather than blind us to your eternal truths. In Jesus' name, amen.

Questions for Reflection

✳ Will you commit to not talking about the ceremony at least three days out of seven? If so, which days?

✳ What act of service can the two of you do in the coming months, before the wedding ceremony? Is there a small group you can participate in? Is there a joint ministry you can support? Is there a grandparent who needs a weekly or monthly visit? Write out a list of service activities that you can do together.

✳ Choose one area of righteousness where you need to grow. Maybe it's humility—putting others first. Maybe it's kindness—initiating good deeds to bless others. Maybe it's patience—not being harsh with others and their weaknesses. How do you want to be spiritually stronger on your wedding day than you are today?

7

STOP WITH THE SECRETS

"Speak the truth to one another."

ZECHARIAH 8:16 (ESV)

A young, single writer once asked me for my best marital advice. I told her, "Married couples have got to stop with the secrets."

I'm not a fan of most dictionary definitions of *intimacy*. They fall far short of the biblical view, so let me offer my own: "Marital intimacy is knowing, accepting, and moving toward each other."

It *begins* with knowing. You can't accept someone you don't truly know. Marriage won't soar on any other basis. If you marry someone you don't know and who won't let you get to know him or her, you can't accept that spouse. If you don't know and accept your spouse, you can't move toward him or her. You end up shadowboxing an image, not building a real relationship with an actual person.

Why get married only to hide? Do you really want to hide for the next fifty to sixty years of your life? Even if you wanted to, you won't be able to. Eventually, the truth will come out. If you don't want someone to know all about you, then don't get married.

Here's the positive hope behind that challenge: honesty is something you can choose to achieve, even if you haven't fully embraced it in the past. Since honesty builds the relationship, intimacy is something you can choose to *make* happen rather than just hope it happens.

Men, one of the most common complaints I hear from wives is that their husbands won't let down their guard. The wives feel as if they never really get to know who their husbands are. We men tend to be afraid of letting someone see the real us, worrying that perhaps when they discover who we really are, they might leave us. But our "hiding" often frustrates our wives more than our sins do. Wives would usually rather deal with what *is* than fret about what *might be*.

Indeed, one of the saddest articles I've ever read was about a

Christian leader who committed suicide once he found out his sin was going to be exposed. After his funeral his wife said, "If he had shared that with me, we could have worked through it." Rather than be honest with

his wife, he chose to take his own life, even though his wife said, "I was willing to accept him even with his sin."

Another wife suspected her husband of some serious misconduct. She looked him in the eyes and said, "I'm the kind of woman who will be true to you and who is willing to work through anything with you. And I mean *anything*. All you have to do is tell me. I need to know— are you being completely honest with me?"

The husband said he was but confessed to a much lesser sin than the pattern of grievous sin that was actually going on. Once the truth came out, the wife left him (with much biblical warrant to do so). She could work through anything, she said, except the lying. There can be no intimacy if there is no honesty.

So, I'm asking the two of you, before you pledge your lives to each other, to sit before God and ask, "Is there anything I need to share with my future spouse that I haven't?" Let this be a holy moment. It is an act of generous love when a prospective spouse discovers a personal challenge about you and still agrees to marry you. It is an act of cruel fraud when you ask someone to pledge his or her life to you while hiding a serious issue.

> **Marriage is the constant exchange of honesty. If there's no real honesty, there's no real marriage.**

If you can't be fully honest with each other, you're not ready for marriage. That's like agreeing to play football—as long as no one hits you. That's like taking a job at McDonald's—as long as you don't have to serve meat. It makes no sense. Marriage is the constant exchange of honesty. If there's no real honesty, there's no real marriage.

Why is honesty so important? God calls himself "the truth"

(John 14:6). If you push the truth out of your marriage, you are pushing out God. It's this aspect of God being truth and us living in God that led Paul to exhort, "Do not lie to each other, since you have taken off your old self with its prac-

tices and have put on the new self, which is being renewed in knowledge in the image of its Creator" (Colossians 3:9–10). Deuteronomy tells us that "all who act dishonestly, are an abomination to the LORD your God" (25:16 ESV). If that's true in business, how doubly true is it in marriage, when you're asking someone to invest his or her very life! When making a list of the ways we should act toward one another, Zechariah began with, "Speak the truth to one another" (8:16 ESV).

So, as you prepare spiritually to become one, ask yourself, "Have I been completely honest with my future spouse? Is there an addiction that he [she] deserves to know about before I ask him [her] to commit to me? Is there something in my past that could influence what I do as a spouse?" (perhaps past abuse, fears, or psychological issues).

I was working with a couple where a secret needed to be shared before the engagement. The person with the secret was terrified of confessing it, but once it was done, the couple's relationship reached a new level of joy and intimacy. He was now able to look forward to their wedding day with joy and anticipation instead of fear and the dread of wondering, *What will happen when she finds out?*

Some guidelines to think about: what you speak can't be unspoken, so don't respond to this devotion in a rash manner. If you have something to share, talk it over beforehand with an experienced believer, pastor, or counselor. Details aren't always helpful. If you have been sexually active in the past, for example, a future spouse deserves to know that, and to what extent. He or she doesn't need to know the intimate details, but frankly, does deserve to know if there were a dozen people or two.

If you suffered past abuse that could impact your freedom of sexual expression; if there is an addiction or habit that could impact your ability to be intimate (and pornography will eventually do that); if there is a huge financial issue; if there is a health issue; if there is anything else that you would want to know about if you were the one on the other side, *share it.* Be wise about how you share and when you share, but eventually share.

If you are the one receiving this information, remember that you're not married yet. It is not cruel for you to ask for more time to test and process what you have just learned (nor is it cruel for your fiancé/fiancée to do the same in the reverse situation). It may, indeed, be wise to postpone or in some cases even call off the wedding. Yes, that may be embarrassing, but it is foolish to commit your entire life to something just to avoid a season of embarrassment. When you agree to marry someone not fully knowing all the details, it is not an act of cowardice or a lack of character to rethink the commitment once the details are known. You are not obligated to marry anyone, so talk through what you've learned with a trusted counselor or spiritual authority.

The pathway to true intimacy and a spectacular marriage is courageous, honest sharing. Now is a good time to start.

Heavenly Father, you have loved us with a perfect, accepting, grace-filled love, the same love with which we want to love each other. Give us the courage to first be honest before you, and then be honest with each other. Bring to our minds anything we need to share before we get married. Give us the courage to share honestly. Prepare us to receive these secrets. Give us wisdom about how to respond to them. In Jesus' name, amen.

Questions for Reflection

※ On your own, apart from each other, sit before God and then before a trusted friend, searching out whether you need to share something you haven't yet shared.

※ Together, discuss how difficult it is for you to tell the truth. What about your upbringing makes it hard to share secrets? Why might you be particularly afraid of letting someone get to know you? Understand each other's personal challenge to honesty. We all struggle in this area, so help your future spouse learn why it's difficult for you in particular.

※ Discuss the best way to express honesty as a couple: when, where, and how. Talk about ways you can foster honesty once you are married: sharing passwords, not being defensive in the face of personal questions, and so forth.

※ Is there an area where you wonder if your future spouse is not being fully honest with you?

8

THE ENTHUSIASM FACTORY

In humility value others above yourselves,
not looking to your own interests but each
of you to the interests of the others.

PHILIPPIANS 2:3–4

There's a very subtle form of pride that most people don't identify as pride, even though it's ruinous to marriage: *we naturally think our marriages will be happier if our spouses would become just a little more like us.*

This is a despicable lie, almost the very definition of pride, and it impacts virtually every aspect of marriage.

Couple A has a woman who likes to resolve arguments immediately and get them over with. She is tempted to resent the fact that her man wants and needs time to reflect on what he's feeling and thinking before being able to talk. It causes her stress that things remain unresolved for even a short period of time; it causes him stress that she's pressuring him toward an artificial resolution before he can comprehend what the issues are.

I just wish he were the type of man who could immediately talk things over, she thinks. *It would cause me so much less stress, and life would be so much easier.*

I just wish she were the type of wife who could just let things simmer for a while, he thinks. *We always work it out in the end. Life would be so much more enjoyable if she just had a little more patience.*

Couple B has a man who would like sexual relations at least every other day. He's married to a woman who thinks once a week would be fine. *Life would be so much better,* he thinks, *if she wanted sex more often.*

Life would be so much better, she thinks, *if he could just be happy with a special Saturday night.*

Rather than seek to find the middle, we naturally want to bring our spouses over to our side of the issue, regardless of what the issue is.

The spiritual challenge of marriage isn't simply accepting each other, but *accepting each other's differences, and even showing enthusiasm for them.* In fact, enthusiasm is one of the best gifts you can give your future spouse: not only accepting each other's differences, but admiring them, celebrating them, eagerly learning from them and being thankful that your life together will be that much richer and more well rounded because the two of you are different.

Let me give you an example from my own marriage. Lisa and I look at food through two radically different lenses. I eat primarily because I hate being hungry, but food isn't something I get all that excited about. It's a means to an end for me. Lisa, on the other hand, likes being hungry because that means she gets to eat. So when we travel, she researches the restaurants and then wants to discuss where I'd like to eat before we go. (She's very into healthy, organic food, which takes a little more effort to find.)

The problem is, I have to work at making myself care. I don't have much natural interest in restaurant reviews or menus, and the fact that it's "local" doesn't mean hardly anything to me, but if I tell Lisa, "Just choose whatever sounds best to you," I spoil her fun. She wants me to at least try to sound excited, to show a little enthusiasm (and even to care that the food is sourced locally).

So, loving my wife means listening to her read the reviews, looking at menus, and trying to be as enthusiastic as possible. When I ran the Houston marathon recently, I ran past a place advertising "organic, locally raised, grass-fed beef." I made a mental note and made sure to mention it to Lisa later that day.

I think this same principle of showing enthusiasm holds true for some couples in regard to sex. For some people, sex is a wonderful, sensual, fulfilling, and thrilling experience. For others, it occasionally may feel like a need, but why all the bother? Let's just do it, get it over with, and move on.

When you're married, if your future spouse enjoys sex the way my spouse enjoys food, and you're more like me when it comes to choosing a restaurant, it's simply a matter of kindness to play along and add a little enthusiasm. Maybe your spouse knows something you don't. I'm not proud of my attitude toward food, and you shouldn't necessarily be proud of your attitude toward sex. I could easily make my lack of interest sound spiritual—eating is often called a sensual desire, it's setting our hearts on transient things, Jesus even warns about giving what we eat too much attention—and you could make those exact same arguments against too much focus on sex.

But here's the thing: Lisa actually serves our marriage by making us care a little more about food and menus than I do. She just about fell into despair when she found out that while I was on a solo trip

to a very small town, I ate at a Wendy's *three days in a row* ("I like the chili," I explained, "and it was close to my hotel"). And perhaps your spouse is serving your marriage by trying to make the sexual relationship more of a "gourmet" experience than you would otherwise enjoy.

Look: it's not healthy for me to eat at a Wendy's three days in a row just because it's convenient and meets the need. And sexually speaking, you don't want "fast food" three times in a row either. So maybe you need a reminder. It would thrill Lisa if I took the initiative occasionally and researched a great restaurant, surprising her and delighting her that for once, she didn't have to do all the work. And it might thrill your spouse if you put a little forethought into an intimate encounter that required a little preparation and effort.

When you discover these differences, remind yourself that having someone who values arriving on time and someone who is more spontaneous and struggles with being late balances each other out. If one is too serious and one is too "fun," or if one is meticulously clean and the other thinks life is too short to spend time cleaning, realize you'll never fully come over to your spouse's side, but you can *appreciate*, *learn from*, and *respect* your spouse's side. The messy person shouldn't resent his or her spouse's request to clean up a little better. Accept it. Even better, *celebrate* it and *praise* it. You know in your heart of hearts being neat and clean is a good thing, right? Maybe your future spouse takes it too seriously, but do you take it seriously enough?

Do you see how this works?

What I love about this is that serving my wife means caring about something that doesn't naturally have all that much appeal to me. Choosing enthusiasm thus creates humility, generosity, kindness, and the spirit of service. These are good things. Isn't this the kind of person you want to become?

> Choosing enthusiasm creates humility, generosity, kindness, and the spirit of service.

And what do we foster when we choose not to care and not to be enthusiastic? Apathy. Self-centeredness. Stinginess. Closed-mindedness.

How you treat your spouse is building a particular character.

If you're a young couple, learning to be enthusiastic about something you're not naturally all that excited about will serve you very well as a parent with your children (who may end up being very different from you and enjoying different things). It will help you in social situations with strangers. It will assist you as your parents get older and want to talk about their days.

Enthusiasm is a wonderful gift for all of life, and marriage is an ideal "factory" out of which it can be liberally produced.

Want a serviceable definition of *marital humility*? Instead of always trying to make your spouse become more like you, consider trying to become a little more like him or her.

———— ∞ ————

Heavenly Father, thank you for making each one of us different from the other. Help us to see your joy in bringing different people together to learn from each other, support each other, and balance each other out. Save me from the pride that wants to remake my spouse in my own image. Help me to appreciate [him/her] just as [he/she] is. In Jesus' name, amen.

———— ∞ ————

Questions for Reflection

✳ What three things first come to mind when you consider how you and your future spouse are different people?

✳ How can you learn to appreciate someone even when you see his or her difference as a weakness (for example, being tardy instead of on time, messy instead of neat, etc.)?

✳ Discuss how the two of you can raise more well-rounded children by being different. What will each of you bring to the parenting process that perhaps the other one lacks?

9

PLEASURE IS YOUR FRIEND

You who are young, be happy
while you are young,
and let your heart give you joy
in the days of your youth.

ECCLESIASTES 11:9

Like a plant or a person, a marriage needs to be fed. One of the most important ways to feed your marriage is with fun and pleasure.

In my book *Pure Pleasure* (Grand Rapids: Zondervan, 2009), I tell the story of an excruciatingly hot run on an August afternoon in Houston, Texas, well before I moved there. About two miles into the run, I thought I was going to collapse into a thirst-induced coma.

When I ran by a half-empty bottle of Coke lying in a ditch, I *actually paused*. It was beyond gross to contemplate, but at least it was wet.

You can't fall that far, Gary, I told myself and kept going, leaving the Coke bottle behind.

Then I came across a family with young children playing in the front yard. I saw they had a hose and asked the mom if I could turn it on for a quick drink. She was very gracious, but I was embarrassed, so I drank it right away without letting the water run all the way through, and it was, as you might guess, disgusting. Who knows how long that water had sat inside that hot plastic tube?

> Instead of focusing on the moment of temptation, focus on what makes you vulnerable to temptation.

Even so, it was wet, and I drank it down because my thirst was monumental.

Writing now, in an air-conditioned room, with a bottle of Fiji water nearby, I'm appalled at the thought of drinking from a hose in front of a house. But rather than fault myself for not having the willpower to say no on a hot run, I think the wiser question would be, *Gary, why did you allow yourself to get into a situation where you were so thirsty that something that should have been repugnant to you actually became a temptation?*

That's the attitude you should build in your marriage. *Instead of focusing on the moment of temptation, focus on what makes you vulnerable to temptation.* If I had been fully hydrated and was carrying a cold bottle of electrolyte-laced water, I wouldn't have even noticed the Coke in the ditch, and I would have run right by the house with the hot hose in front.

When you stop having fun in your marriage, you become

relationally thirsty. The Bible urges you to "enjoy life with your wife, whom you love" (Ecclesiastes 9:9). Things that wouldn't even be

a temptation to you when you're connecting with your spouse suddenly seem tantalizing when you can't remember the last time you laughed together. Never stop enjoying each other.

Think of this as a delightful promise: the decision to get married is a decision to keep having fun together! You're promising that you'll make each other's enjoyment a priority. I see so many marriages that become "utilitarian"—that is, they're all about taking care of the house, the kids, work, and so on. People get bored with their lives, and then they get bored with each other, and then they want out.

Don't let this happen to you. If the moment ever comes when you can't remember the last time the two of you laughed, take this as a "spiritual doctor's" prescription: go do something fun in the next three days. If you notice you're running out of date-night ideas, invite another couple along—it's okay to laugh with another couple. Forget about work and pressure and bills, and resolve that you are going to enjoy this marriage.

Here's a startling fact: I once read that more than 80 percent of husbands who cheat on their wives want to return after the affair is over. You know what that tells me? The problem was never the women they were married to, or else they'd never want to come back. *The problem was the state of the relationship.* They had let it become utilitarian. They stopped having fun. The affair was about getting away, rediscovering sexual intimacy, laughing with someone, and doing something other than work or child-rearing.

You can do that with each other! You don't have to have an affair with someone else because you're bored. Have an affair with your spouse.

In any given marriage, there is typically one partner who is more focused on having fun. If you're not that spouse, thank God that he has given you someone to help keep you from being overly serious. But don't be lazy in return. Realize that you also need to plan fun things to do as a couple.

Within the safe confines of marriage, pleasure will be one of the truest friends and protectors of your relationship. Use this God-given tool to build a temptation-proof marriage. Your commitment to a lasting union is actually a commitment to enjoy each other for the rest of your lives. Here's to a life of laughter, fun, and delight.

------ ∞ ------

Heavenly Father, your goodness and kindness are seen in this: amid work, service, and sacrifice, you call us to enjoy each other and to laugh together as husband and wife. You created us as the only creatures truly capable of laughter, because we are the only creatures made in your image. You command us to take a day off, and your Word celebrates us enjoying each other. Help us to embrace this good, abundant life, and remind us if we ever become overly serious that it is dangerous to remain "relationally thirsty." Unleash the creativity of your Holy Spirit to guide us to new times of laughter and fun and sexual delight. In Jesus' name, amen.

Questions for Reflection

✳ In many couples, there's one partner who is better at making sure the two of you have fun on a regular basis. Which partner is that for the two of you? Will you both agree that taking time away to have fun is a wise and good thing to do?

✳ What are two or three of your favorite things to do together? Plan at least two new, fun things to do in your first year of marriage.

✳ What do you think is most likely to keep the two of you from having fun in the future? What kind of reminder can you give yourselves to not let fun times die?

10

THE WORK OF MARRIAGE

Whatever you do, work at
it with all your heart.

COLOSSIANS 3:23

Marriage brings with it many blessings, joys, and even occasional ecstasies. But there's a hard truth about marriage and family life: it can sometimes be a ton of hard work. "Those who marry will face many troubles in this life" (1 Corinthians 7:28).

Especially if you raise kids together, you may find yourself more exhausted than you have ever been. You will vaguely remember the romantic dates of long ago when the two of you laughed without worry, spent money without care, and returned home to a quiet, soft bed.

Hopefully, you'll still have date nights, but now those nights will likely be a budget item, and you may feel a little guilty spending the money. You will be tired from a long day, and you'll have a difficult time mentally leaving your kids behind. And you will almost never come home to a quiet house.

Even if you don't have kids, being married is very different from dating. You need to make sure you have the groceries you need, the bills are paid, and your house is cleaned. You will now need to stay connected not just to your extended family, but also to your spouse's extended family. And your circle of friends nearly doubles, requiring more obligations, phone calls, and visits (more weddings, birthday celebrations, office parties, etc.).

If you don't prepare yourself for the work of marriage—if you don't anticipate that the joys of marriage bring with them increased responsibility—you might begin to resent your marriage. You may initially feel this as resentment toward your spouse, but often it's resentment over the fact that life and marriage can be difficult.

If you notice more "toil and trouble" after marriage than before, it doesn't necessarily mean you married the wrong person—it may just be a consequence of leaving singleness behind. You've made a huge commitment to another person, and that necessarily requires additional responsibilities—something that would be true regardless of who you married.

The apostle Paul said, "A married man is concerned about the affairs of this world—how he can please his wife—and his interests are divided. An unmarried woman . . . is concerned about the Lord's affairs: Her aim is to be devoted to the Lord in both body and spirit. But a married woman is concerned about the affairs of this world—how she can please her husband" (1 Corinthians 7:33–34).

Never make the mistake of blaming your spouse for the work of life and marriage. That would be as silly as opening up a store and resenting the entrance of every customer.

Enjoy the playfulness of dating, the fun and romance of the honeymoon, and the anticipation of sharing life together. Seize these seasons and future joyous ones as they come and go. Enjoy and relish them. Thank God for them. But also prepare yourselves spiritually by remembering that there are also other seasons up ahead—seasons of sacrifice, seasons of service, seasons of self-denial, and seasons of work.

> If you notice more "toil and trouble" after marriage than before, it doesn't necessarily mean you married the wrong person—it may just be a consequence of leaving singleness behind.

A real marriage is three-dimensional. Sometimes, we become enamored with one or two dimensions, but the reality is, life isn't always easy, so marriage isn't always easy.

Rich? Yes.

Easy? No.

―――――― ∞∞∞ ――――――

Heavenly Father, prepare our hearts for the work of marriage. Let us never resent each other or even resent our lives when things get difficult. Help us remember that this is a fallen world that has many joys and happiness, but also much heartache and even heartbreak. Thank you for enabling us to live in this world and face these challenges together. In Jesus' name, amen.

―――――― ∞∞∞ ――――――

Questions for Reflection

※ Each of you talk about your parents' marriage. Did you notice the work that was required in their relationship? How did they handle it? What can you learn from them? What can you do better?

※ What greater responsibilities do you think being married will lay on you that you don't now have to carry?

※ Be honest with yourselves and each other— do you willingly or even eagerly embrace hard work, or do you tend to feel sorry for yourself when life gets difficult? How challenging do you think the work of marriage will be for you personally? What can you do now to prepare for it?

11

INTOXICATED WITH PASSION

Eat, friends, and drink;
drink your fill of love.

SONG OF SONGS 5:1

Earnest believers who have faithfully abstained from sexual relations before marriage, or who fell but recommitted to abstinence, can sometimes have a difficult time fully giving themselves over to the freedom of sexual expression in marriage. They feel guilty. After years of telling themselves no, they have a hard time letting go and enjoying the passion.

God doesn't tell us to say no to sex outside of marriage because it's inherently dirty or repugnant, but because sex is so wonderful and powerful that its expression should only be unleashed in the context of a lifelong covenant. What it does, spiritually and physically, in our hearts and souls, our brains and bodies, is so remarkable that marriage is the only safe place for its power to be fully unleashed.

Arm yourself with Scripture to understand just how pro-sex God is. Consider this: as important as prayer and charity are to the Christian life, there isn't a single book in the Bible devoted exclusively to either. When you think about it, there is only one book in the Bible with one central focus, and that's the *Song of Songs*—an unflinching, unashamed celebration of erotic love between a husband and wife.

Do you understand what the phrase "Song of Songs" means? It's an ancient Near Eastern idiom that exalts something above all else. For instance, you've heard of "King of kings," haven't you? Such a phrase signifies that God isn't just *a* king or even the strongest of all kings. It means that if you were to gather all the kings of the world together, God would still be the King of the kings. He isn't just superior; he is different in kind, one step above.

So, the Bible describes the erotic relationship of husband and wife as, not just one of the best human experiences, or even a particularly intense human experience, but rather, the human experience above all human experiences. Think about what sex does: it unites husband and wife in a spiritual way. It refreshes their affection for each other in a physical way. It sets up the potential to create another human being—a child in your image! It reminds you that you are a physical being with physical nerve endings that can fire away, as well as a spiritual being whose soul is being knit to your spouse in a unique and profound way.

The mere *title* of one biblical book tells us so much about God's celebration of marital sexuality.

Proverbs 5:18–19 celebrates sexual love play:

> *May you rejoice in the wife of your youth.*
> *A loving doe, a graceful deer—*
> > *may her breasts satisfy you always,*
> > *may you ever be intoxicated with her love.*

That word "intoxicated" is so strong that one commentator described it as a "morally permissible love ecstasy." It captures the image of a man who is all but struck dumb at the sight of his wife's naked body—he is captivated by what he sees. And notice this is in the form of a blessing—it's not shameful; it's God's will.

> If you are a woman, the mere sight of your naked body may make your husband weak and will give you a certain power over him—a power that God designed for you to have.

If you are a woman, the mere sight of your naked body may make your husband weak and will give you a certain power over him—a power that God designed for you to have. Don't fear it or be ashamed of it. Use it to enthrall your husband and enjoy being desired. It's a good thing for your husband to fill his eyes with you, and for you to revel in the hold you have over him, part of God's marital engineering, if you will.

Elsewhere in the Song of Songs, God himself notices the husband and wife enjoying each other and said, "Eat, friends, drink, and be drunk with love!" (5:1 ESV). This passage actually celebrates "feasting" on our passion for each other, even to the point of feeling as though we are "intoxicated" with our desire for each other. Within marriage this is a good, holy, and healthy thing.

Marriage and family can be exhausting and at times even tedious. In the midst of these seasons, God has given us something better than getting drunk on alcohol or high on prescription drugs as a means of escape—he has created physical passion between a husband and a wife, a passion so intense that it can make us momentarily forget money troubles, parenting concerns, sometimes even health-related problems. For a brief interlude we are intensely focused on each other, what we are feeling, what we are enjoying. And the neurological effects of that experience often pave the way for a really good night of sleep.

Understanding all this, is it so surprising that God encourages us to give way to our passion, to "feast" on our lovemaking and be "intoxicated" by our desire for each other? God, who created the Sabbath, knows the value of rest. Marital sex can be a form of rest in the midst of daily responsibilities, heartache, and tedium.

If you think accepting the sacredness

of sexuality might be a challenge for you, prayerfully read through the Song of Songs before your wedding. It is a very appropriate and holy prayer to respond to these scriptures by asking God to give you the same openness to sexual pleasure and unbridled enthusiasm for sexual intimacy that you see modeled in the Bible. Understand that as soon as the pastor says, "You may kiss the bride" and you walk down that aisle, you and your spouse can share far more than a kiss. Your covenant has opened the door to a lifetime of sexual passion and enjoyment.

It could be very special, a truly holy and sacred moment, if you take time to pray before you first consummate the marriage. Thank God for the gift you are about to receive, ask his blessing for a future lifetime of sexual pleasure, and ask him to give you an open mind and heart and body to receive this gift, without guilt or shame. Then give yourselves to each other, fully and without reservation, shame, or guilt. Embrace the pleasure, thank God for the sensations, and enjoy the favor of God's creative genius.

Heavenly Father, we thank you for the gift of sexuality within marriage. Prepare our hearts to receive it, to enjoy it, and to celebrate it. Help us overcome any feelings of shame or repugnance; help our hearts and minds to shift from saying no to sexual passion to saying an enthusiastic "yes!" We want to fully enjoy and embrace all aspects of marriage as you have designed it. In Jesus' name, amen.

Questions for Reflection

❋ Do you expect that you'll struggle with accepting the holiness of marital sexuality? Why or why not?

❋ If you think this might be a challenge, consider reading Clifford and Joyce J. Penner's *Getting Your Sex Life Off to a Great Start* (Nashville: Thomas Nelson, 1994) or Dr. Douglas Rosenau's *A Celebration of Sex: A Guide to Enjoying God's Gift of Sexual Intimacy* (Nashville: Thomas Nelson, 2002). Women will find much practical help by reading various articles on Shelia Wray Gregoire's blog (https://tolovehonorandvacuum.com) or by perusing Dr. Juli Slattery's and Linda Dillow's website, www.authenticintimacy.com.

❋ Talk about how you can make the wedding night a special spiritual as well as physical experience as you embark on a lifetime of sexual intimacy.

12

THE VERY BEST GIFT

———— ∞∞ ————

I keep asking that the God of our Lord
Jesus Christ, the glorious Father, may give
you the Spirit of wisdom and revelation,
so that you may know him better. I
pray that the eyes of your heart may be
enlightened in order that you may know
the hope to which he has called you,
the riches of his glorious inheritance in
his holy people, and his incomparably
great power for us who believe.

EPHESIANS 1:17–19

The very best gift you can give your spouse, spiritually, is a gift that will serve you even more: help your spouse draw closer to God and learn to draw from his presence on a daily basis.

Ninety percent of the changes and attitudinal adjustments in my marriage haven't come from my wife confronting me. They came about after a time of prayer when my heavenly Father convicted me, reminded me that I'm married to his daughter, and insisted on change. From that point on, it was about God and me even more than it was about Lisa and me.

Nagging doesn't work, for wives or for husbands. In the history of marriage, you won't find one marriage relationship dramatically impacted in a positive way by frequent nagging.

But conviction from the Holy Spirit?

That works.

When you encourage and support your spouse regularly meeting with God, he will be your biggest advocate if your spouse gets too busy or distracted or simply starts to lose his or her zeal to be fully engaged in your marriage.

Here's what I've found: the less I receive from God, the more I demand of my wife. The more I receive from God—through worshipping, praying, studying his Word, and opening my heart to his life-giving presence—the more capable I am of loving my wife, the more zealous I am to excel as a husband, and the more willing I am to serve my wife rather than demand from her.

So, the very best gift you can give your future spouse—and yourself—is to help him or her find time and passion to regularly connect with God and to do the same yourself. Inspire each other to draw ever closer to God. Make time during the week, on weekends, and even on your honeymoon to spend quality time cultivating a heart for God and enjoying his presence. Resolve that you'll be active members of a local church community that will regularly inspire you to make room in your life and heart for God.

Marriage requires a new spiritual maturity. It will make new demands on your character. It will call you to a new selflessness. It will challenge you in new ways. It will reveal hidden weaknesses. Once you are married, you will need God more than you ever have before, but that's okay because he is an able Source, a trusted Friend, a powerful Ally, an empathetic Comforter, and a light in the darkness. It is crucial, if you want a great, life-giving, and soul-satisfying marriage, that you pursue God with a new passion, and learn the secret of life in Christ—not as a religion, an obligation, or a guilt trip, but as a way to draw from a personal, living source who wants to love your spouse through you.

> **It is crucial, if you want a great, life-giving, and soul-satisfying marriage, that you pursue God with a new passion.**

In your first year of marriage, I'd recommend you read through my book *Sacred Pathways: Discover Your Soul's Path to God* (Grand Rapids: Zondervan, 2010). We don't all connect with God in the same way, and *Sacred Pathways* will help you understand the way God made you so that you can craft

a "quiet time" or devotional time that fits who you are.

You might be a traditionalist and will meet God most effectively with time-honored rituals and practices. You might be an intellectual and will find your heart most awakened when you learn new concepts or truths about God. Perhaps you're a naturalist—who meets God best out of doors—or a sensate, who enjoys bringing all five senses into play when you worship. There are several other types to explore.

Understanding your own spiritual temperament (or "sacred pathway") will help you write a "prescription" to more intentionally meet with God and receive from him. Understanding your spouse's temperament will assist you in giving your spouse the time and space he or she needs to surrender both heart and mind to God. Giving your spouse time to connect with God, and encouraging him or her to pursue God more and more, is one of the most gracious, loving, and wise things you can do as a spouse (and it will end up greatly serving you as well).

Your marriage will be better served when God becomes an ever-growing influence in your life. He will help you love others more. He will enable you to lay aside the petty sins and motivations that bring so many marriages down. He will supply more patience, gentleness, courage, humility, and generosity—all of which will greatly bless your union.

God's presence is the greatest untapped source of strength in marriage. Too many couples settle for a once-a-week (or less) church service, a perfunctory personal "prayer" time, and leave it at that—just enough to not feel too guilty about it.

If you take the time to meet with God regularly, you will find, as I have, that you crave it more and more, particularly when you feel free to craft a time with God that fits who you are. As you seek to draw ever closer to each other, recognize that the most powerful way to do that is to first draw ever closer to God and let him provide the grace, motivation and love that will lead you to a more intimate marriage.

———— ∞ ————

Heavenly Father, you are the source of all joy, strength, love, and life. We want you to fill us more and more so that you become the center of our marriage. Give us a thirst to pursue you and make room for you in our lives. Help us to discover how we best meet with you. Draw us to you with a new passion as you draw us to each other. In Jesus' name, amen.

———— ∞ ————

Questions for Reflection

* If you were to describe your current passion for meeting with God on a regular basis on a scale of 1 to 10 (with 1 being no desire at all and 10 being white-hot), what number would you give yourself?

* List three ways that regularly meeting with God could radically transform the way you treat each other, and how it could bless your marriage.

* What can you do in the first year of marriage to put this principle into practice? Will you be intentional about finding a solid church that will help you grow? Might you consider getting a copy of *Sacred Pathways*?

13

DON'T BELIEVE THE LIES

⬡

"The devil . . . was a murderer from the
beginning, not holding to the truth,
for there is no truth in him. When he
lies, he speaks his native language, for
he is a liar and the father of lies."

JOHN 8:44

Before your wedding and after, Satan will lie to you, frequently and creatively. He probably even lied to you today.

Jesus calls Satan "the father of lies," and if you don't want him to murder your marriage, you have to learn how to discern those lies.

Satan takes normal marital doldrums and turns them into the story of your life. "It won't get better; it can't get better. Your only hope

is to kill your marriage." Jesus says Satan "steals, kills, and destroys" (John 10:10, paraphrased), so whenever you hear "kill" as a solution, you know who you're listening to.

Satan will tell you your spouse "never listens" to you because he or she ignored you once. He will tell you your spouse is "always" selfish at the end of what may admittedly have been a selfish day. One of his favorite tricks is to take an act and paint the entire person and all of his or her history with that one act.

Satan not only lies about the problem; he also lies about the "solution." He will suggest a coping strategy that you know would disappoint your spouse, and then he'll suggest you lie about it. Since you can't be intimate with someone you're lying to, he's tempting you to engage in a form of marital sabotage. If you'd be ashamed doing something in front of your spouse, that's a good reason to never do it, even when your spouse isn't there.

Satan also lies to take away your base of support and peace. In his nineteenth-century classic, *The Christian in Complete Armour*, William Gurnall warned that when Satan is ineffective in getting us to *sin*, he works on getting us to *fret*. "It is easier to keep flies out of your pantry in the summer than to keep Satan's servants from stealing your joy and infecting your peace."[1] If you develop a mental narrative about your marriage and/or your spouse that robs you of joy and peace, you should at least consider that it might be a spiritual attack.

When you hear a lie and don't confront it, it becomes your "truth," even though it's not true—which means we have to be constant and expert lie detectors. Fight back, with vigor:

"My spouse had a bad day, but he's not a bad spouse."

"My wife can be a little self-absorbed, but remember how she spoiled me last week?"

"We're not all that great when taking vacations together—but we do so well ministering together."

"Maybe our sex life isn't the best it's ever been, but we still enjoy each other and we can work on that. Couples have faced much worse."

> **Whether you want to or not, you will have to engage in spiritual warfare if indeed you want to build and maintain a magnificent marriage.**

To get married is to enter a new spiritual arena with new spiritual vulnerabilities. Whether you want to or not, you will have to engage in spiritual warfare if indeed you want to build and maintain a magnificent marriage. Seek out Satan's lies, expose them, and kill them before they kill your joy, if not your marriage.

Jesus, we know you won the victory over Satan. Just as you taught your disciples to be wary of his lies, so you warn us to be aware that he will try to attack our marriage with lies, half-truths, and distortions. Give us submissive hearts and minds that are in tune with Scripture and your still, small voice so that we become more aware of your counsel and better detectors of Satan's deceit. You promise us that your sheep will hear your voice. Help us to hear it more clearly, now and certainly after our wedding. In Jesus' name, amen.

Questions for Reflection

※ Try to think of a time that a lie was sown in your mind—it could be in your current romantic relationship, or with another friend, or a parent—and discuss how it impacted your relationship negatively until you discovered the truth.

※ What lies are you letting masquerade as truths in your current relationship? What ones do you need to weed out before marriage? How do you think they may come back after you're married?

✳ Since Satan is the father of lies and Jesus calls himself the truth, any time you lie to each other you are declaring your spiritual allegiance. Will you pledge to be absolutely truthful with each other, now and in the future?

14

MARRIAGE IS A TEAM SPORT

Make every effort to add to your faith
goodness; and to goodness, knowledge;
and to knowledge, self-control; and
to self-control, perseverance; and to
perseverance, godliness; and to godliness,
mutual affection; and to mutual affection,
love. For if you possess these qualities in
increasing measure, they will keep you
from being ineffective and unproductive in
your knowledge of our Lord Jesus Christ.

2 PETER 1:5-8

During the 2016 Summer Olympics, the US volleyball team of Kerri Walsh Jennings and April Ross lost a rough semifinal match to the Brazilian team. Walsh Jennings, the most decorated female Olympic beach volleyball player ever, wasn't having her best day, so the Brazilian team kept targeting her, directing most of their attacks her way. In a stunner, the US team lost in straight sets—the first match Walsh Jennings had ever lost at the Olympics.

To her credit, Walsh Jennings took responsibility and said she just had to start playing better (which she did; she and Ross went on to win the bronze medal).

Marriage is kind of like beach volleyball. There are two players per side, and the team can be only as strong as the weakest player. If one partner has a persistent weakness, the marriage will suffer accordingly.

In Frank Shorter's autobiography, *My Marathon* (New York: Rodale, 2016), Frank shared how at any elite marathon there are only about ten runners physically capable of winning. The 1972 Olympic men's marathon was delayed a day due to the terrorist attacks on the Olympic village. The runner who had the fastest time in the world that year was having lunch with Frank and complained that the delay would be catastrophic—their training was carefully calibrated, and pushing the race to a different day would mess everything up.

Frank was far more laid-back, responding, "Hey, we've been training for this race our entire lives, and one day shouldn't make that much of a difference." He added to the reader that at that point he knew this guy—even though he had the fastest time in the world that year—wasn't going to win the gold medal. He had already talked himself off the podium before the race even started.

As I read this account to Lisa, she said, "That's you!"

"I know!" I responded. "But I want to become more like Frank Shorter."

My marriage will improve when I learn to roll with the changes, not obsess over things I can't control, and refuse to think the worst when unexpected interruptions occur. As long as I allow myself to be obsessive in a negative way, our marriage will suffer and my own joy, peace and confidence will be shattered.

So, as you prepare to be married, think about that personality trait that isn't what you wish it were. If you don't address it, that's where your marriage will suffer. Remember—you're like a beach volleyball team. If you are responsible financially but your spouse isn't, your marriage may still hit the financial rocks. If you are Eeyore and your spouse is Tigger, your marriage will suffer the effects of your negativity or impulsivity. Once you get married, you no longer stand alone—everything you are and aren't will impact your marriage, either positively or negatively.

> Once you get married, you no longer stand alone—everything you are and aren't will impact your marriage, either positively or negatively.

The beach volleyball metaphor of marriage means that one of the best gifts you can give to your spouse after the wedding is a

commitment to keep growing in the Lord. If you cling to romantic sentimentality ("Why can't he love me just the way I am?"), you're preferring spiritual laziness over the health of your marriage and over the desire to bless your spouse. I have the opportunity to give my spouse a gift—a better, more mature me—and I don't want to become too selfish or too lazy or grow too comfortable with her acceptance when I might be able to bless her with my transformation.

In his Word and by His Spirit, God has made available to us everything we need to grow: "His divine power has given us everything we need for a godly life through our knowledge of him who called us by his own glory and goodness" (2 Peter 1:3).

Which means not growing *is a choice*. If you are a Christian and you want to grow, you can.

Where do you need to grow? Where is your marriage threatened by a personal weakness? Start preparing yourself spiritually now, even before the wedding, by addressing those areas where you are weakest.

Heavenly Father, I thank you so much that my future spouse is willing to receive me just as I am, but help me to grow so that I become ever more mature. Give me the desire to surrender to you, to pursue a holy life, so that I will not be the weak spiritual link holding our marriage back. Thank you for the wonderful promise that in Christ and your Word, you have given me everything I need to grow. In Jesus' name, amen.

Questions for Reflection

✻ How does addressing a weakness as a team differ from the way you faced personal weaknesses as an individual?

✻ What is the "weakest link" that you're bringing into this marriage? How can you begin addressing it now?

✻ Discuss with each other the best way to gently encourage each other toward greater maturity and growth. You don't want to nag each other or tear each other down, so discuss the best and healthiest way for your future spouse to lovingly share areas where he or she thinks you can grow.

15

THE GUILT OF "TEMPTING ANOTHER SOUL"

Jesus said to his disciples: "Things that
cause people to stumble are bound to
come, but woe to anyone through whom
they come. It would be better for them to
be thrown into the sea with a millstone tied
around their neck than to cause one of these
little ones to stumble. So watch yourselves."

LUKE 17:1-3

M y wife loves to play Boggle, and she's really good at it, which
is why few people want to play her. But on her birthday and

Mother's Day, and usually at least one evening during a holiday, her family joins her.

Our love for her calls us to join her in her great love.

Lisa also loves to bike, which is why I bike a lot more than I probably would otherwise. I prefer to run. But Lisa's love for biking makes me much more of a biker.

That principle—we do what our spouses love and like to do—is fine when it comes to hobbies. It is spiritually deadly and poisonous when the same principle is unleashed by our sins.

If you hold on to a sinful attitude, there will come a time when you will want your spouse to join you in that sin.

Marriage contains within itself the power of glorious good—encouragement, support, enthusiasm, love, service, loyalty. It gives us the tools to bless one particular person in a way we can bless no one else. But this potential comes with a sinister side—it also offers a platform for temptation. If we abuse the platform, we can do great and serious evil.

When we allow sin to remain, we can't fully contain it any more than we can confine an oil tanker spill. Sin spreads widely and chaotically by its very nature; it multiplies beyond our control (the more we give in, the stronger its hold on us) and therefore makes those closest to us most vulnerable.

The challenge is that no

one—not a single soul—is exempt from sometimes fierce temptation. To live is to be tempted. Sometimes we will fall, and when we do, we will be grateful for God's grace and remedy in Jesus. But one aspect of temptation, particularly as it relates to marriage, that we need to be especially careful about is *not dragging our spouses into the temptation.*

Old-time preacher Clarence Macartney once said,

> However much we have been marred and scarred by the tempter's shafts, let us at least see to it that ours shall not be the guilt of tempting another soul. If in hell there are gradations of punishments, as the words of Jesus about few and many stripes would seem to indicate, then hell's severest retributions must surely fall upon the souls of those who have deliberately and malignantly tempted other people.[1]

How do we tempt our spouses?

If you are a liar, you will eventually ask your spouse to lie to cover up your sin. You may even ask him to lie to one of his dearest friends or nearest relatives. Perhaps you'll ask him to lie to a government official. When you do that, you have entered a new level of evil and are abusing the intimacy of marriage.

If you cherish a sexual sin, the time will likely come when you will ask your spouse to join you in that sin. It will no longer be sufficient to merely get lost in a fantasy of thought—you may want to live it out. And your spouse, predisposed to please you and enjoy you, will feel more intense temptation even though the sin may be something she never would have thought of on her own. This is a serious betrayal of the marital bed and the marital bond.

If you are negative or a gossip, you will try to draw your spouse into speaking critically of others, or make your spouse feel less than thankful for the good things God has given him or her. Instead of leaving church satisfied by the worship, you will point out that one sentence the pastor said

> You cannot accommodate sin without endangering your spouse.

that could possibly be taken the wrong way. Instead of making your spouse grateful for how God has provided, you will be a constant drip of negativity for how everything in your house or car or life isn't quite "perfect" and you can't be content until everything is, in fact, perfect.

These are just three examples— you can supply your own. But the thought alone should be enough to make us pursue holiness for the sake of our spouses. I hate my sin, and I hate how I am tempted—I'm sure you do as well. The last thing I want to do is take something I hate and make it a part of my precious wife's life as well.

You cannot accommodate sin without endangering your spouse. Your apathy toward growing a heart that is a bulwark against sin is tantamount to a man who, out of laziness, neglects to even close the door of his house while he is away, inviting all to enter as they wish.

One of the reasons we bought our particular house in the Heights is that it has a locked wall around it. The outside gate is a stout door; the other side is behind a tall, barred fence (the Heights is in the urban part of Houston, so crime isn't all that uncommon, unfortunately). Every time I leave the house in the morning while Lisa is still inside, I lock both the inside doors and the outside doors. I have no peace of mind until I know my wife is safe behind at least two formidable barriers.

But how foolish would it be to lock physical doors while leaving spiritual ones open? How stupid would it be to protect our house from physical theft while leaving Satan a highway into my wife's heart and soul through my own weakness?

Don't accept in your own soul that which could poison your spouse's. It's not just about you. As soon as you get married, your personal pursuit of holiness (or lack of it) it will have major consequences for your spouse.

———————— ∞ ————————

Heavenly Father, I want to help my future spouse grow closer to you every day. The last thing I want to do is tempt my spouse to fall away from you. Do a deep spiritual work in my heart and soul so that I will not pass my current temptations on to my spouse. Help me to gain victory and help me to be vigilant. In Jesus' name, amen.

———————— ∞ ————————

Questions for Reflection

✳ List one or two of your current temptations that are most likely to influence or tempt your future spouse. Ask each other what you think those temptations might be.

✳ Will you invite your future spouse to pray for you in this area and perhaps to even hold you accountable? Discuss what this would look like.

✳ Is there someone you could talk to, or a book you could read together, that could help you in your vulnerable areas? Will you consider setting up an appointment or ordering that book right now?

16

PRIME EXAMPLES

Let us purify ourselves from everything that
contaminates body and spirit, perfecting
holiness out of reverence for God.

2 CORINTHIANS 7:1

Have you ever considered how few verses there are in the Bible telling parents *how* to parent their children? It's really quite astonishing when you think about it. You can find hundreds of books suggesting someone has discovered "God's method" for raising kids, but you'll be hard-pressed to find more than just a few verses in all of the New Testament, and not that many more in the Old.

There's a message behind this silence: the Bible's view of influence comes from example more than from recipes, and the Bible is neither silent nor sparing on that subject. Wives are told to be examples to their husbands (1 Peter 3:1). Jesus' form of discipleship was "I have set you an example that you should do as I have done for you" (John 13:15). Paul told the Corinthians to follow his example as he followed Christ's (1 Corinthians 11:1). He told both Timothy and Titus that pastoral leadership consists largely of setting an example for everyone under their care (1 Timothy 4:12; Titus 2:7).

Your future children, should God bless you with any, will be under

your spiritual care. Even if you don't have biological children, if you are faithful as a believer, you will have spiritual children you encourage and minister to, so you need to strive to become the best example you can be, beginning *now*. That's the biblical model out of which influence grows.

There is a sense in which making a marital commitment forces us to grow up or at least grow deeper. By no means am I calling singles carefree and selfish—not even close—but making a commitment such as marriage, where one person is immediately impacted by our actions and habits, and creating the opportunity for potential future children, who will be equally impacted by who we are, can certainly be a sobering call to maturity.

This call to influence others is behind Paul's call for us to purify ourselves from "everything that contaminates body and spirit" (2 Corinthians 7:1). "Purifying" ourselves begins, of course, with receiving Christ's grace and forgiveness. But it doesn't stop there, because Paul added (in the present tense, mind you, signifying an ongoing action) "perfecting holiness out of reverence for God."

> If you bring prejudices into your marriage, you are likely to bring down your spouse.

Holiness is something we "perfect." We'll never be done growing. We'll never master all our bad habits or always do the right things we want to do. But Paul was equally adamant in suggesting that pursuing such holiness should be every Christian's goal.

If you bring prejudices into your marriage, you are likely to bring down your spouse. You may raise racially (or class-based) prejudicial children. Instead of spreading the message of God's reconciling love, you will foster a household of hate and discrimination. You can't hide a heart of disdain. Your future children will notice the way you speak, look, act, and treat others.

Men, if you have a naturally negative view of women, or women, if you have a naturally negative view of men, and neither of you deal with that before your marriage, your relationship will suffer enormously, and your kids will be hindered that much more from having healthy relationships with their future spouses.

If your spending habits aren't under control; if you have health issues resulting from an unhealthy relationship with food; if you don't care for your body; if you are a proud person or a greedy person or an unkind person, all of these foibles will negatively impact not only your marriage, but your future children.

Many of these things can't and won't be surrendered overnight. You can find out you are expecting a child in seven months and still have plenty of time to prepare a nursery, procure a crib, buy a few baby clothes, and make the necessary physical arrangements to bring a baby into your life. But seven months isn't nearly long enough to unseat prejudice, hatred, self-loathing, addictions, or laziness.

Think about the kind of mom or dad (physical or spiritual) that you want to be. Where do you need to grow in order for that vision to be realized? If you're bold, ask each other: "Where do you think I need to grow? What do I need to change? What good habits need to be developed, and what bad habits need to be crucified?"

Spiritual preparation for parenthood should begin *right now*, so help each other get started. Just as working out in a gym can build fun intimacy, so encouraging each other to grow spiritually will do the same. It's not about "gotcha" spirituality, where we catch each other failing and then pour on the shame. It's about mutual encouragement birthed in grace, understanding, and forgiveness.

Make this an exciting pursuit: train to become a person who's a "prime example."

Father God, we want to become the kind of couple that is a force for your good in this world. Help us to be prime examples of love, grace, integrity, honesty, and service. Should you bless us with children, we want to model with our lives all that you teach us to say with our tongues. In Jesus' name, amen.

Questions for Reflection

❋ What are the top two negative habits that you think you need to address before getting married or becoming a parent?

❋ What positive characteristics or virtues do you want to see more of in your life?

❋ How can you help each other "perfect holiness out of reverence for God"? Discuss the role of grace, accountability, and encouragement.

❋ Describe the kind of parent you want to be someday. Now talk about how to get there.

PART 2

PREPARING FOR
YOUR VOWS

———— ∞ ————

V ows matter.

Even if we don't carefully think about what we're saying, God holds us to them. And traditional wedding vows are so packed with meaning that thoughtfully considering them and talking about them ahead of time can make your wedding day all the more momentous.

The rest of this devotional is designed to help you think through every line of the traditional vows so that when you utter them, you will have thought about exactly what you are promising to do. First, we'll go through the "statement of intent," and then we'll explore the actual vows. The goal is that you will have prayed through, thought about, and discussed what each word in these very important vows means, preparing you for this choice and making the choice that much more meaningful and powerful.

You may choose not to use the traditional vows in your wedding, but even so, using them to prepare your heart and soul for the wedding can bless you greatly.

THE STATEMENT
OF INTENT

———— ∞ ————

Will you take this woman to be your
wedded wife, to live together after
God's ordinance, in the covenant of
marriage? Will you love her, comfort
her, honor and keep her in sickness
and in health; and forsaking all others,
keep yourself only unto her, so long as
you both shall live? If so, say, "I will."

17

THE GIFT YOU ARE ABOUT TO RECEIVE

⌒∞⌒

"Will you take this man to be
your wedded husband . . . ?"
"Will you take this woman to be
your wedded wife . . . ?"

Your future spouse is about to give you the most precious gift imaginable: his or her very self. It still overwhelms me, thirty years into my own marriage, that my wife gave (and is giving) herself to me, without limit. She has placed her hopes and dreams of happiness at risk, as they are impacted by how I speak to her and treat her. She is vulnerable if I become disabled, and she must care for me. She freely gives her body, her time, her counsel, her warmth, her intellect, and her comfort to me on a daily basis. And she has now been doing this for more than three decades!

God forbid that I ever take this for granted.

Ever.

I want to reward that gift, not treat it as though she's handing me a stick of gum: "Oh, thanks."

It doesn't become less of a gift as the years pass, something I can now take for granted. It becomes even more of a gift. I want to be like the apostle Paul, who said of the Philippians, "I thank my God every time I remember you" (Philippians 1:3).

Remind yourself: *nobody has to marry me.* That's right; none of us *deserve* someone giving us a lifelong commitment. That's why the statement of intent begins with, "*Will you* take this [man/woman] to be your wedded [husband/wife]?"

Now that you have found someone who *is* willing to do this, respond by giving everything you have and everything you are back to that person (from the wedding day forward). Withhold nothing. No activity, no hobby, no past associations (other than God, of course) matter as much as your future spouse's welfare and happiness. Your future children may give you great joy, but they will eventually leave.

For the rest of your life, this one person comes first.

There is only one person who is committing to stand by you in sickness and poverty, to meet your sexual needs, to make you the first focus of his or her care. That's huge. That's almost unbelievable.

> **Remind yourself:** *nobody has to marry me.* **That's right; none of us** *deserve* **someone giving us a lifelong commitment.**

Yet that's what you two are about to give to each other.

When an employer asks you for your top loyalty, remember that no one can come above your spouse—even the person who can fire you. When a charity wants you to volunteer your time and money, do it with the blessing of your spouse, or not at all.

If you truly understand the immensity of this gift of someone always putting you first, your initial words after you kiss and walk down the aisle should be, "Thank you. Thank you. *Thank you.*"

And your first resolve on the morning of your very first full day of marriage?

"I will spend the rest of my life continuing to thank you for the incredible gift you gave to me yesterday when you pledged to me your very self."

Heavenly Father, open my eyes, heart, and mind to better understand the wonder that another person has agreed to give everything to me—their future, their hopes, all their resources, their very body. Let that never become old or routine. Give us truly thankful hearts now and on our wedding day, and help us live with gratitude for this amazing gift. In Jesus' name, amen.

Questions for Reflection

❋ Talk to each other about the best gift anyone has ever given you up until this moment. Now compare that with the gift you will give each other on your wedding day.

❋ What can you do to remind yourself of the gift you are going to give to each other, so that it doesn't become routine?

18

THE JOURNEY FROM "ME" TO "WE"

⎯⎯⎯ ∞∞ ⎯⎯⎯

"... to live together after God's ordinance,
in the covenant of marriage ..."

Y ou're about to embark on a journey that could well be described as the journey from "me" to "we." You've lived your entire life (or the bulk of your life) as an individual whose highest allegiance, under God, was to your own path, your own well-being, and your own satisfaction.

That must end in order for the marriage to start. Once you say, "I do," you agree that "we" becomes more important than "me." For the rest of your life, when you face a decision, it has to be placed in the context of "what is best for us *as a couple*?"

This can and will impact where you live, how you live, what you do, how you spend your time, how you spend your money, and where you go to church. You'll bring much strife into your marriage if you begin any day or conversation with "me" instead of "we" as the starting point.

"Let's vacation there because that's what I like to do best."

"Let's move to that place because that's what's best for my career path."

"Let's spend our holidays at this place because that's what I'm used to doing, and I don't want to give it up."

Everything has to be placed in the "maybe" pile. You have to rethink how you spend your money, your evenings, your weekends, and your holidays. You have to rethink priorities for time, scheduling, even meals, bedtime, and where you live. *This is what it means to become one.* To not do this is to invite a roommate into your house rather than a spouse. That gets frustrating because you know in your heart marriage should be a deeper commitment than that.

Let me get practical: I've talked to couples with varying vocational paths. For one couple, the wife earned four times more than the husband. Even so, they knew they wanted kids soon, and that would mean the husband would probably stay home to watch them while he pursued more education to prepare for future job opportunities. When she got an even more promising job offer one thousand miles away, they moved, because that's what was best for their family.

On the other hand, a young couple planned for the wife to stay home with the kids when the kids were young, though they hoped to delay child-rearing for five years or so. On a premarital survey, she marked that both vocational paths—for the husband and the wife— were equally important. After talking about it, however, she realized that for the family's long-term prosperity, it seemed wisest to support her husband first in achieving his vocational goals since there would be a significant season when he might be the only wage earner. This was at first a challenge for her intellectually—she didn't like how it sounded. She didn't ever want to think of herself as a "kept" woman. But being practical, she realized it's what made the most sense. Doing what would be best for her family was more important than holding on to ideals that she thought her peers would value.

> If you don't die to yourself as an individual, you can't be reborn as a couple.

Many of us come into marriage with certain hobbies that also need to be rethought. It's one thing to climb mountains or engage in other dangerous hobbies when you're single, but if someone depends on you, especially if children are involved, you might have to rethink those favorite pastimes. If a single woman spends two hours a day on Facebook to keep up with friends, few will question her priorities. As soon as she's married, and certainly if she becomes a mom, there may not be two hours in the day when that's the best use of her time. Few would challenge a single guy spending every Saturday morning and early afternoon playing a round of golf with his buddies. Once he has small kids and a tighter family budget, those expenditures of time and money might look very different.

Do you see how everything has to be reevaluated? The entire orientation of your life is turned upside down. It's no longer, "What do I want?" but rather, "What is best for *us*?"

Jesus said that unless we die, we can't be reborn to new life (John 12:24). That's also an accurate statement of marriage. If you don't die to yourself as an individual, you can't be reborn as a couple. This is a spiritual reality, requiring a shift in your thinking, your feeling, your attitude, and your prayers.

If you're generally a self-centered person, you'll want to make this a matter of concerted prayer before the wedding. Talk this over with each other and with trusted believers; let others speak into your life. This is a key spiritual skill that has to be mastered, if indeed you want to build a monumental marriage.

⌀⌀⌀

Father God, we desire the kind of marriage where "we" becomes more important to us than "me." This is what most glorifies you, and this is the kind of marriage that will be happiest, so we ask that you do a work in our hearts to put our self-centeredness to death and help us begin to rethink how to apply this truth. Show each of us where we tend to put ourselves first. Help us find joy in making what may feel like a personal sacrifice but will actually be best for us as a couple. Give us a new vision of what it truly means, spiritually, for two people to become one. In Jesus' name, amen.

———————— ∞∞∞ ————————

Questions for Reflection

✳ What do you think will be most difficult for you to put on the chopping block once you are married? Will it be a hobby, how you spend your money or your time, where you spend your holidays? Where do you expect to struggle most?

✳ Will you allow other couples into your life so you can talk through conflicting desires with them? How will the two of you figure out what is best for you as a couple when you both want different things? Talk about some people you can approach for discernment and advice.

✳ Think about placing a scripture or a simple statement (such as, "Marriage is the journey from 'me' to 'we'") where you will see it every day—where you get dressed, in your car, in a favorite room of the house—to remind you of the need to die to yourself. What will help you maintain and practice this spiritual attitude?

19

LOVE SERVANTS

∞

"Will you love [her/him]?"

In marriage, it all comes back to love.

Love is exalted by Jesus (John 13:34–35), Peter (1 Peter 4:8), John (1 John 3:11), and most shockingly, by Paul in Galatians 5:13–14, where he said, "Through love become slaves to one another. For the whole law is summed up in a single commandment, 'You shall love your neighbor as yourself'" (NRSV).

If being a "love slave" is our call to a brother or sister on behalf of the gospel, how much more is it our call within the covenant of marriage? I am to become a "love slave" to my wife. Christ has set me free, dealing a serious blow to the sin that rules over me (pride, selfishness, control, manipulation, narcissism), *in order that* I could so serve my wife, be so devoted to my wife, so focused on my wife, and so mindful of my wife, that anyone watching me might consider me her "love slave."

This changes the "game" of marriage entirely. This turns my thoughts away from where my brain naturally wanders: *Why won't my wife do this? Why won't my wife do that?* If I'm her "love slave," why would I even expect her to focus on me? I am called to focus on *her.*

If *two* people do this—both husband and wife—you'll have a prophetic picture of the new life in Christ that speaks so strongly to the world of the presence of God. If even one spouse does it, you'll have what Peter says is the most effective form of marital evangelism (1 Peter 3:1). This isn't natural; it's supernatural. It's not about an infatuation—it's about a divine manifestation, for no one loves like this on his or her own.

> For the rest of your life: if someone were to observe you in your marriage, he or she should think, *It's almost like she's his love slave,* or *It seems like he lives to serve her.*

Here's what you are about to promise, for the rest of your life: if someone were to observe you in your marriage, he or she should think, *It's almost like she's his love slave,* or, *It seems like he lives to serve her.*

A love slave initiates both thought and action; a love slave studies his or her mate to determine what that mate really needs perhaps before he or she even knows it: Is she getting too tired? Is he too stressed? Does she need a day away, on her own, apart from the kids, and even me? Does he need a particularly vigorous lovemaking session? Does he need someone to tell him "No, what you're doing is harmful"? Does she need someone to tell her, "Listen: you can't please everyone; let this go"?

When we define *love* as doing what God thinks is best for our mates, "love slave" loses the dangerous negative connotations (excusing abuse, demeaning behavior, or joining our mates in evil) and becomes an inspiring call to always do what is best for our spouses in order to build them

up in Christ. Paul used strong language, but the man who wrote that husbands should love their wives "as Christ loved the church" would never condone a man abusing his wife (Ephesians 5:25); we know that's not what Paul was talking about.

The world's form of relating is depicted in Galatians 5:15: "If, however, you bite and devour one another, take care that you are not consumed by one another" (NRSV). Biting and devouring one another and "consuming" each other with contempt is an all-too-common horror show in marriage. Instead of viewing themselves as servants, these couples view themselves as prosecutor, judge and jury. The focus becomes, "Fill me, complete me, serve me, pleasure me, pleasure me even more, now more still, and don't ever tell me no."

You are promising to *love* and to *comfort* your spouse. Both of those are active, initiating verbs. It implies that you are thinking about your spouse's welfare and then acting on it when something comes to mind. It also assumes you are focused on fulfilling your

responsibilities more than you are thinking about how your spouse is treating you.

The best kinds of marriages aren't built on casual love; they're built with each partner thinking of himself or herself as a "love slave" to the other. That's the shocking commitment you are about to make.

Our heavenly Father, you have loved us so well. Please grant us the grace to love each other with a similarly shocking kind of sacrificial love. We're not promising to be roommates or colleagues; your Word calls us to a much higher commitment, to be love slaves to each other. Ready our hearts and minds to fulfill this pledge. In Jesus' name, amen.

Questions for Reflection

❋ Have you witnessed any marriages that model this kind of "love slave" mentality? If so, talk about it.

❋ You could argue that the opposite of love isn't hate but rather apathy. How can you avoid becoming passive in your relationship, to ensure that you *actively* love and comfort each other?

❋ How close have the two of you already come to this kind of love? What do you think you can do to draw even closer after the wedding?

20

MUTUAL CARE

⚬⚬⚬

"Will you comfort him/her?"

I have a tendency to wake up ridiculously early, often even before 4 a.m. I'll try, many times unsuccessfully, to go back to sleep. One morning I just gave in and got up.

An hour or so later, walking out of my office, I saw the master bedroom light was turned on from underneath the door. That meant Lisa was up, and it wasn't even five o'clock yet. She never gets up that early, so I opened the door. Lisa told me she was also having trouble getting back to sleep, so she was trying to do her Bible study. It was difficult to feel alert without her coffee, but she didn't want to drink coffee because that would guarantee she wouldn't fall back asleep.

I turned off the lights and said, "Let's go back to bed. I'll curl up with you, and if we're not asleep in thirty minutes, we'll get back up."

I knew I wasn't going back to sleep (and soon got up again), but

> **Marriage is about "comforting" each other.**

I also knew that taking those ten minutes, lying by Lisa's side, would put her back to sleep (which it did). I knew her day would go better if she got more sleep, so I took the opportunity to help make that happen.

Why?

Marriage is about "comforting" each other.

At the very genesis of marriage, God proclaimed, "It is not good for the man to be alone" (Genesis 2:18). God doesn't want us to have to face the normal challenges of life without someone to help us. The Bible builds on this thought in the book of Ecclesiastes:

> *Two are better than one,*
> *because they have a good return for their labor:*
> *If either of them falls down,*
> *one can help the other up.*
> *But pity anyone who falls*
> *and has no one to help them up.*
> *Also, if two lie down together, they will keep warm.*
> *But how can one keep warm alone?*
> *Though one may be overpowered,*
> *two can defend themselves.*
> *A cord of three strands is not quickly broken.* (4:9–12)

In your marriage vows, you are promising to bring comfort to your spouse. We married folks know that if our spouses need more sleep, we want to help them sleep. If they are hungry and need to be fed, we want to help them get fed. If they are discouraged and need encouragement, if they are threatened and need a protector, if they are overworked and need someone to help them relax, well, that's what we signed up for—and now, that's what *you* are signing up for: to be your spouse's comforter in exactly those moments.

—————— ∞ ——————

Heavenly Father, how kind of you to give us each other for our mutual comfort. Help make us unusually sensitive to each other's needs, and give us the empathy, discernment, and motivation to comfort each other in the midst of those needs. In Jesus' name, amen.

—————— ∞ ——————

Questions for Reflection

❋ Have you had many opportunities yet to comfort each other? Talk about those times when you felt most comforted by your future spouse.

❋ Discuss how you both can become more sensitive to when the other needs comfort; what are your personal cues that the other needs to watch out for?

21

THE HIGHEST PLACE

"Will you honor [him/her]?"

T o honor someone is to single him or her out. You say, "This person is different; this person is special; this person deserves to be recognized."

In your wedding vows you are promising to keep honoring your spouse as special throughout your life, to have the following attitudes, exhibited in the Song of Songs:

Husband to wife:

"My dove, my perfect one, is the only one." (6:9 ESV)

Wife to husband:

"My beloved is radiant and ruddy, outstanding among ten thousand." (5:10)

When you honor someone, you give that individual the "seat of honor"—the preferred place. On the day you exchange your vows and sign your name on the wedding license, you're committing for the rest of your life to put one person ahead of every other person in your life—over your parents, over your childhood best friends, over your future children, *even over yourself*. Second only to your passion and loyalty for God, your passion should burn brightest and your loyalty be most closely guarded for your husband or wife. To honor your parents or children over your spouse is to dishonor your spouse and break your vows.

In a sermon entitled "The Duties of Husbands and Wives," famous evangelist John Wesley wrote:

> The wife is to have the highest place in the husband's heart, and he in hers. No neighbor, no friend, no parent, no child, should be so near and dear to either as the other. . . . They must do more, and suffer more for each other, than any other in all the world . . . the husband must do or leave undone, anything he can, that he may please his wife . . . in diet, attire, choice of company, and all things else, each must fulfill the other's desire as absolutely as can be done, without transgressing the law of God . . . Helpful fidelity consists in their mutual care to abstain from and prevent whatever might grieve or hurt either.[1]

> **Second only to your passion and loyalty for God, your passion should burn brightest and your loyalty be most closely guarded for your husband or wife.**

Does anyone *not* want a marriage like this, two people so in tune with each other and each so dedicated to the other's welfare that nothing else will come between them save the presence and will of God? I think all of us would, in an ideal world, desire such a marriage.

You *can* build such a marriage. The biggest challenge may not be a friend or parent—it may be your own loyalties.

I was watching a playoff football game on a Sunday afternoon, and my wife mentioned that she had to return a painting to a home goods store. The store is in downtown Houston, which means she would have fought traffic if she tried to return it midweek. Lisa is more than capable of driving, but she enjoys herself so much more going downtown or shopping if someone does the driving for her, so I put the game on pause and took forty-five minutes to drive her there and back.

"Why?" you might ask. Because it honored her. It made her day a little sweeter. That's all the reason I needed. That's what I believe it means to be married. I honored her above my own pastime.

Notice Wesley also mentioned that we must "abstain from . . . whatever might grieve or hurt either." I trust this makes it clear that any kind of physical violence or intimidation has no place in marriage—absolutely none. Not even once. The same is true with unkind words, whether they are spoken in front of your spouse's face or behind his or her back. If something will hurt your spouse with no healing purpose (which completely forbids physical violence of any kind), it has no place in marriage. That kind of activity is *dishonoring*.

The word *honor* is a brilliant addition to the marital promise. It's a commitment to make your spouse feel special, revered, and to hold him or her above all others, including above your work, family and friendships, hobbies and self-interests. Honor means resolving to do what makes life sweeter for each other while avoiding anything that will cause harm. In this way you'll build and preserve a very happy marriage indeed.

———————— ∞ ————————

Heavenly Father, do a deep work in our hearts so that we favor each other over anyone or anything else, out of reverence first and foremost for you. Give us the desire to make each other's lives a little bit sweeter, even if that means denying others or ourselves. Keep us from ever doing each other any harm. In Jesus' name, amen.

———————— ∞ ————————

Questions for Reflection

❋ As you look ahead to your wedding day, which existing relationship has the most potential to come between you and your spouse: a parent, a sibling, a friend?

❋ What passion do you need to make secondary in order to make your marriage primary?

❋ Is there any pattern of hurting each other in your current relationship? Be honest with each other—is there something that your future spouse does that you find hurtful or dishonoring? Have the courage to mention it, and then address it further if it doesn't immediately stop.

22

BROKEN BODIES

⎯⎯⎯∞⎯⎯⎯

"... in sickness and in health ... ?"

S usannah Thompson was initially less than impressed by the young Baptist preacher named Charles Spurgeon, but she was soon won over by his charm and demeanor. When Charles eventually declared his love for her, Susannah rapturously praised God "for His great mercy in giving me the love of so good a man. If I had known, then, how good he was, and how great he would become, I would have been overwhelmed, not so much with the happiness of being his, as with responsibility which such a situation would entail."[1]

Responsibility, indeed. Though a great preacher, Spurgeon had a fragile body and, in one sense, an ailing mind. When he was just thirty (eight years after they married), Charles began suffering from horrendous bouts of gout, an excruciatingly painful condition that in his case came with another crushing ailment: depression.

Susannah knew she was marrying a man who had a special gift from God, but she didn't know she would need to stand by a man with a painful physical ailment and a potentially debilitating mental ailment in a day and age when medicine was of little help to either.

Charles was likewise smitten by Susannah on their wedding day, January 8, 1856. He and his new bride must have conceived a child on or near their honeymoon, because Susannah gave birth to a set of twin boys on September 20 of that same year.

Susannah never fully recovered from the birth. That birth was followed by other physical ailments that kept her bedridden or housebound—on one occasion for a fifteen-year stretch. Charles preached to an overflowing church building in which, for more than a decade, his wife never once set foot.

Since pregnancy affects a woman's health in the very first trimester, Charles pledged to marry a woman who was in robust health but who, *just weeks later*, would *never* be that healthy again.

Yet Charles and Susannah had a loving and intimate union. Here are two letters Charles wrote to Susannah, both from the year

1871.[2] Notice the affection Charles obviously had for Susannah in spite of the physical challenges that assaulted both of them:

My Own Dear one—None know how grateful I am to God for you. In all I have ever done for Him, you have a large share. For in making me so happy you have fitted me for service. Not an ounce of power has ever been lost to the good cause through you. I have served the Lord far more, and never less, for your sweet companionship. The Lord God Almighty bless you now and forever!

And later that same year:

I have been thinking over my strange history, and musing on eternal love's great river-head from which such streams of mercy have flowed to me. . . . Think of the love which gave me that dear lady for a wife, and made her such a wife; to me, the ideal wife, and, as I believe, without exaggeration or love-flourishing, the precise form in which God would make a woman for such a man as I am, if He designed her to be the greatest of all earthly blessings to him; and in some sense a spiritual blessing, too, for in that also am I richly profited by you, though you would not believe it. I will leave this "good matter" ere the paper is covered; but not till I have sent you as many kisses as there are waves on the sea.

> **You are committing to marry a real person, with a real and fragile body, and to stand by him or her, in sickness and in health.**

Sickness needn't destroy a marriage, but it will severely challenge a marriage unless both husband and wife enter their union with the full commitment that they will stick together regardless of what physical ailments assault their joy. You are committing to marry a real person, with a real and fragile body, and to stand by him or her, in sickness and in health.

Heavenly Father, we don't need to know the future because we know you've already gone there before us and will provide us the grace to meet whatever challenge we may face. Help us to take full advantage of our days of health—to enjoy each other, to serve you and others, and to relish the blessing of vitality and strength. But as we enjoy these times, prepare our hearts to stay true if our bodies or minds should begin to break down. In Jesus' name we pray, amen.

Questions for Reflection

❋ Share some things you'd like to do while you have the good health to enjoy them. How can the two of you be good stewards of whatever health situation you are in now?

❋ Knowing that your spouse is committing to be there "in sickness and in health," what changes do you need to make in your lifestyle (eating, exercising, sleeping) in order to be a good steward of your health and not unnecessarily burden your future spouse?

❋ Discuss ways that the two of you can encourage each other toward healthy living.

23

RADICALLY CONNECTED

⚭

"And forsaking all others, keep
yourself only unto [him/her]?"

W hen we think of betraying our wedding vows, we usually
think of something sexual, but there's a far more common
betrayal that isn't about romance or sex; it's about relational connection that may not even be romantic. *Being closer to anyone other than
your spouse is a betrayal of your wedding vows.*

The object of your affection might be a child, a parent, or a best
friend for whom there is no romantic connection at all—but if there
is more intentional and invested intimacy in that relationship than
there is in your marriage, it crosses the line into betrayal. This doesn't
mean you can't have occasionally intense "therapeutic chats" with
a good friend or relative (though such conversations are extremely
unwise if the chat is with someone for whom you could develop a

romantic attraction, especially if your marriage is in a weak place). Marriage isn't to be your only relationship, but it *is* to be your primary relationship.

When you promise to "forsake all others and keep myself only unto you," you're making a sexual promise (that should be absolute) but also a promise about emotional relationships. You'll put each other first.

Every marriage that wants to mature must move toward holding each other dearer than all others. That may mean, sometime in the future, occasionally enduring a short season of loneliness until the relationship is restored. When you face a "barren season" of marriage, or a particularly busy season (every marriage has them), you may be tempted to find greater intimacy with a friend or a child to ease the painful distance you feel from your spouse. *That's exactly when your vows to forsake all others will matter most.* A promise isn't necessary when it's not tested; it's when it's difficult to keep that it matters most.

> Marriage isn't to be your only relationship, but it *is* to be your primary relationship.

If you find a temporary substitute, you won't seek as urgently to be restored to your spouse. In time, the temporary substitute becomes a permanent crutch, and you get used to living in a distant marriage. This is a constant temptation, as it will feel easier sometimes to revert to substitute intimacy—your former best friend, a parent or sibling, a future child—rather than do the relational work to stay connected to your spouse. But that will encase your relational distance in cement, leading to a subpar marriage.

At this stage in your relationship, I'm sure you desire an abundant

marriage. Such a marriage takes a lot of vigilance and perseverance: "Let us not become weary in doing good, for at the proper time we will reap a harvest if we do not give up" (Galatians 6:9)

You have to keep planting good things in your marriage—plentiful and intentional times of all aspects of intimacy; and you have to keep weeding—pulling out any substitute that may be sucking the life out of your relationship or getting in the way of your exclusive need for each other.

Don't let a hobby, a sin, a friend, or even another family member ever become nearer and dearer to you than your spouse. You are about to promise each other that for the rest of your lives, you will never seek to be closer to anyone other than the person you are marrying. Anything less is a betrayal of your vows.

∞

Heavenly Father, give me a willing heart to make myself this vulnerable to my future spouse. Let me be committed to being closer to [him/her] than I will ever be to anyone else. Give me an active conscience and

a heart of discernment should there ever be a season
when either one of us begins to drift and depend more
on someone else. Keep this union tight and solid, to the
glory of your name. In Jesus' name, amen.

Questions for Reflection

❈ Do you believe you are ready to make this high commitment—that you will pledge, for the rest of your life, to be closer to each other than to anyone else?

❈ What do you need from each other to make such a commitment? Be practical—what helps you feel closest and most connected to each other? That's what you're agreeing to keep doing.

❈ Are you concerned about any of your future spouse's current relationships overshadowing his or her commitment to you? If so, talk about them. Be open, humble and vulnerable as you consider your fiancé/fiancée's concerns. At this stage, you should be more sensitive to your spouse's concerns—making sure he or she feels secure—than you are about hurting another friend's feelings.

24

TURTLEDOVE LOVE

∞

". . . so long as you both shall live?"

T urtledoves are perhaps most famous for their place in what has become a slightly obnoxious Christmas song: "On the second day of Christmas, my true love sent to me two turtledoves and a partridge in a pear tree . . ."

Outside of this song, turtledoves are known for two things:

- they mate for life (thus you almost always find them in pairs); and
- they have no peripheral vision.

These two realities are connected. Successful mating for life requires a certain tunnel vision.

My own eye condition helps me understand this. A couple of

decades ago, I was diagnosed with keratoconus, a degenerative eye disease that makes your cornea resemble a cone, making everything appear blurry. It has gotten so advanced in my left eye that an ophthalmologist told me I don't really use my left eye. My brain basically relies on my right eye.

It's not a big deal, except when I'm biking or running. Then I have to completely turn my head to see over my left shoulder, but most people live with worse medical maladies than this. There have been a few embarrassing moments, like when I applied for a new driver's license and was asked to read the letters in the "middle" column.

I could see only two columns, and there's no "middle" in two.

"Is there something wrong with you?" my tester asked.

How long did she have?

For a short season, I agreed to try out a contact for my left eye. After years of having no peripheral vision, it felt like a different world.

Walking down a grocery aisle and seeing aisles on *both* sides felt distracting, as if something were coming at me. I was so used to my tunnel vision (plus, I just hated putting something in my eye every morning) that I took the contact out and have lived with my condition ever since. Yes, Lisa hates that I do this, but I'm more comfortable with my malady than I am with the cure.

A similar kind of *spiritual* tunnel vision will serve us in marriage. Successful mating for life requires a certain focus and a ruthless determination to ignore "side views." If you want a fulfilling, turtledove-mating-for-life experience, you can't be distracted by other affections, flirtations, or what-ifs. You can't waste time thinking, *Well, if something happened to my spouse, the next spouse I choose would be more like* that.

> **Successful mating for life requires a certain focus and a ruthless determination to ignore "side views."**

We must look with a singular eye on the marriages and spouses that we have. We must think and act and hope and dream as if the marriages we are in are our only chance at marital happiness.

Because for the vast majority of us, they are.

Being lured away from a turtledove mind-set is one of the subtlest spiritual attacks there is. Most of us would be appalled by actually considering an affair, but "what if" fantasies seem a step removed from actually cheating on our spouses. *I don't want to cheat on my spouse, but what would it be like if I were married to a* different *spouse?* That doesn't sound so sinful because it's not about sex, but it can be hugely destructive to a marriage, and it obliterates a sacred marriage mind-set.

Turtledove tunnel vision preserves and serves marriage by focusing on making the existing relationship better rather than fantasizing about an imaginary one.

By definition, marriage-for-life isn't just a choice to give up all other choices; it's a commitment to give up even imagining any other choice.

On your wedding day, you're going to make this promise: "You are my one true love, for the rest of my life. My best chance for happiness is going to come from learning to love you the best that I can so that we are always in tune with each other. As far as romance is concerned, I will invest all my thoughts and energies on this marriage and this relationship for the rest of my life."

Every time you hear "The Twelve Days of Christmas" at a mall, on the radio, or at a coffee shop, let it be a reminder that as far as your marriage is concerned, the most important day is the second day, the turtledove day.

Heavenly Father, we are so grateful to have found someone to commit our lives to, to focus on, and to cherish until the day one of us dies. Give us new focus and determination to stay true to this marital "tunnel vision." In Jesus' name, amen.

Questions for Reflection

✻ Discuss how much it means to you that your future spouse is agreeing to focus his or her affection on you, and to make you a top priority, for the rest of his or her life.

✻ Consider buying a turtledove picture or Christmas tree ornament so that every Christmas season, you can be reminded of the commitment you are making to each other.

PART 3

THE WEDDING VOWS

———————— ∞ ————————

I, _____ take thee,
_____, to be my wedded
husband/wife, to have and to hold from
this day forward, for better for worse,
for richer, for poorer, in sickness and in
health, to love and to cherish, until we are
parted by death. This is my solemn vow.

25

OWN YOUR CHOICE

———— ∞ ————

"I take thee to be my wedded
[wife/husband]."

What I am about to say has been considered somewhat controversial. Normally, I'd try to avoid controversy in an inspirational book like this, but the point is particularly well worth making at this stage in your life.

In general, God doesn't, and won't, tell us who to marry. We don't see in Scripture that it would be disobedient not to marry any one particular individual. There is no command in the Bible that says, "You must get married." And there is certainly no command, "Greg must marry Susan."

God is a sovereign God, and it is wise to seek his guidance, but that doesn't mean he promises to tell us the exact person we should marry. On your wedding day, you are making a choice. The best platform on

which to build a monumental marriage is one in which you own this choice instead of putting it off on God.

In 1 Corinthians 7:39, the apostle Paul asked widows to consider staying single (explaining that it's their choice whether they want to marry again or not) and then told them that such a woman is free to marry "anyone she wishes" as long as her potential husband "belongs to the Lord."

If the Bible explicitly says, "It's your call whether or not to get married" (a sentiment Jesus echoed when he said some "choose" to become eunuchs—that is, live a celibate life—in Matthew 19:12, with emphasis on the word "choose") *and* it's entirely your choice as to who to marry, this tells us that a marriage choice is part of God's permissible will.

In other words, he lets us choose.

Is it *possible* God has told a couple to get married? Look: I'm not going to put God in a box. I can't say, "He can do this but he can never do that." All I can say is that the clearest scriptural teaching makes marriage our choice—both as to whether we get married and to whom we marry. Presuming that you've somehow identified "the one" and can therefore ignore clear biblical teaching is risky and foolish.

While the Bible is silent on how you can definitively know who you're "supposed" to marry, it does talk about the process of making wise decisions—applying biblical principles, seeking wise counsel, being deliberate and wise in your choice, considering the future, and basing your decision on the right priorities. That's a better foundation on which to base a lifelong marriage than trying to second-guess some divine design.

Why does this matter?

To excel in marriage, we have to own up to our choices—why we made them and how to be responsible in the face of them. I have seen way too many couples enter into a difficult season of marriage and then blame God for "making" them marry the spouses who seem to be causing them so much pain. They treat God as their enemy, just when they need him to be their truest friend.

Also, the virtues of kindness, faithfulness, and goodness demand that if I convince someone to marry me, or agree to marry someone, *knowing* it is a lifetime commitment, *knowing* it would be beyond complicated to dissolve the union, I need to step up to face the lifetime consequences. That means not just staying married but staying *engaged* in the marriage, working to make it the best for my spouse that I can.

> To excel in marriage, we have to own up to our choices—why we made them and how to be responsible in the face of them.

Spiritually, I want you to accept the clear teaching of Scripture: "Whether I get married is up to me. Paul and Jesus both say singleness can be a legitimate choice. And Proverbs 31 as well as 1 Corinthians 7:39 clearly teach that I get to choose the kind of person I want to marry. So, I'm making this choice in freedom. You are the person I want to, and choose to, marry."

In a way, this is more romantic, not less. Revel in the joy of this spiritual reality! Look each other in the eyes and say, "I choose you! God says I can choose anyone, but I don't want anyone else. I want you. For the rest of my life, I choose you."

Resolve in your mind, *I am making a choice. And I will honor this choice. And I will follow up this one choice with thousands of other choices to make it the best choice I have ever made.*

———∞———

Heavenly Father, thank you for giving us the freedom to choose who we spend this life with. I thank you for the circumstances that led us to meet, and I thank you for the wonderful gift my future spouse is giving me by choosing to marry me. On our special day when we get married, I realize I am making a choice. Prepare my heart to be faithful and true to that choice. In Jesus' name, amen.

———∞———

Questions for Reflection

❋ In what ways does it sound even more romantic that God freely lets you choose to marry whomever you wish?

❋ Why do you think it is important to "own" your choice about who you're marrying? How might this affect the way you work at marriage?

❋ Talk about why you think marrying each other is a particularly wise choice for each one of you.

26

ONE FLESH

∞

"... to have and to hold ..."

From a Christian perspective, perhaps one of the most dramatic differences in moving from a dating/engaged couple to a married couple is freely sharing your bodies with each other. If you've already been sexually intimate, may I invite you, for your own spiritual welfare and future marital happiness, to stop until the wedding day?

The Bible is rather clear about sex before marriage. There are about two dozen passages in Scripture that speak against "sexual immorality," and several of these passages are clearly referring to any sexual activity outside of marriage (1 Corinthians 7:1–5 and 1 Thessalonians 4:3–8 are just two examples).

Deliberately and persistently rebelling against God's wisdom and plan for any part of our lives shapes us into a certain kind of person. We become "Dalmatian Christians"—accepting the Bible "in spots," wherever it suits us. We essentially become our own gods, each following the true God where we care to and ignoring him if there's ever a disagreement between our desires and his will.

Since you're engaged, there's a definite ending to this physical "fast." Why not decide, from this day forward, to submit to God and let him remake your heart into an obedient one? It's not as though he's telling you to go without sex for the rest of your life. He simply teaches us that we should wait for marriage.

When Jesus gave us God's perspective of marriage, he did so with stark language. Using Genesis 1:27 and 2:24 as a basis, he said, "'For this reason a man will leave his father and mother and be united to his wife, and the two will become one flesh.' So they are no longer two, but one flesh. Therefore what God has joined together, let no one separate" (Matthew 19:5–6).

Jesus combined the thought of spiritual and physical oneness. He lifted the sex act ("be united") out of the realm of recreation—it's not like dancing or wrestling or even holding hands—and filled it with spiritual meaning. Sexual intimacy is a powerful, profound threshold to an amazing spiritual reality that expresses oneness in marriage, not merely mutual interest.

Before you say, "Well, that's *your* interpretation," the truth is it's actually the way the *apostle Paul* interpreted Jesus' words as well. He used the *same* Genesis passage Jesus referred to when warning people away from prostitution in 1 Corinthians 6. If sex were just about a physical activity, why would prostitution be considered wrong, provided you paid a fair wage? Yet Paul wrote, "Do you not know that he who unites himself with a prostitute is one with her in body? For it is said, 'The two will become one flesh.' But whoever is united with the Lord is one with him in spirit" (vv. 16–17).

Some might say that of course God has a problem with adultery, but is it really adultery if you're not married yet? But Hebrews 13:4 says, "God will judge the adulterer *and* all the sexually immoral" (emphasis added), meaning that there is sexual immorality apart from adultery. The Christian church, for almost its entire history, has held no other view of sex before marriage. There will always be a few outliers, of course, but no major Christian tradition has ever accepted that engaging in sexual activity outside of marriage is something that Christians can do with a good conscience.

To be spiritually prepared for marriage is to seek purity before God. For God to be a bigger part of your marriage, he has to be a bigger part of your life.

> **For God to be a bigger part of your marriage, he has to be a bigger part of your life.**

If you've already stumbled in this area, you can't undo what you've done, but you can receive God's pardon and grace and let his Holy Spirit redirect your hearts toward obedience from this point on. *This process must begin with accepting God's truth as your truth.*

And yet I see so many couples do the reverse: their sex life is most active and most exciting before they get married, and it often dies within a few months or a couple of years after the wedding. That seems so sad—but it makes spiritual sense. If we disobey God before the wedding—"I'm going to have sex whether he wants me to or not because I want to"—it only makes sense that we won't obey God to make sex a richly enjoyed, generous activity after marriage. We didn't respect his prohibitions before marriage, so why would we value his recommendations after marriage?

One of the great problems of promiscuity is that it sets us off course spiritually. When we knowingly disobey God, we create habits of disobedience that can lead us astray in many other areas. If we never confess and repent,* it's like entering marriage with one protective wall torn down. The next spiritual assault can come in unimpeded. It may be financial temptation. It may be another sexual temptation. It may be related to food or entertainment. But if we knowingly disobey in one area, we've developed hearts that are at least somewhat callous to God's conviction. That's the attitude and spirit that can destroy us and our marriage. For a soul-satisfying marriage, you want to be *more* sensitive to God, not less.

Surrendering to God is the most self-serving thing you can do because God has your best interests in mind. He wants you to have a magnificent marriage and a magnificent sex life. Sin makes us miserable. If we were best served by sex before marriage, God would

---

* *Repent* means to stop doing what is wrong and start doing what is right. It is a change of mind and heart that leads to a change of action—a new disposition to surrender to God's will in all things.

command us to have sex before marriage. When he says to wait until marriage, that's evidence enough that it's best for us to wait.

So, if you've messed up, where's the way back? This is key: healing doesn't come from denial. Just repressing the fact that it happened, or pretending that it doesn't really matter, won't remove its sting. And if you keep having sex before marriage, you're saying God's will and Word don't really matter. That's one of several reasons why it's so helpful to enjoy a season of obedience before the wedding.

Take some time to do a spiritual inventory. Most of us come into marriage with various degrees of sexual brokenness. The commitment and acceptance of marriage creates the ideal platform for great healing. We can explore the boundaries and passions of sexual love with great freedom and enjoyment, loving each other just as we are.

One of the worst things you can carry into your honeymoon is guilt over your past. Guilt won't serve you in marriage. It won't make you a better lover. It may war against your ability to please your spouse.

Freely repent, confess, and receive God's and each other's forgiveness. Holding on to guilt as an act of penance is not only spiritually heretical (denying the sufficiency of Christ's work when he bought your forgiveness by dying on the cross), but it's physically devastating to your future sexual enjoyment.

Thinking, *But I've sinned before marriage, so I don't deserve sexual happiness in marriage* is a complete misunderstanding of grace. The whole notion of grace is that because Jesus paid the price, we don't have to. Your spiritual debt is marked "PAID IN FULL" when you lay it at the foot of the cross. Holding on to guilt will essentially make your spouse pay for your past sins. Let the sin stay in the past; don't allow it to assault the present or future.

I realize talking about abstaining from sex may seem rather outdated to some of you, even silly to others. But the notion of obeying God—even when it hurts—is never outdated and never silly and always consequential. This challenge gives you an opportunity to enter marriage by submitting the most intimate parts of who you are to the lordship of Jesus Christ. If you will do that, it will positively impact every aspect of your life and certainly your future marriage.

———— ∞ ————

Heavenly Father, sex is your creation and your idea. You know how it works best. Help us, from this day forward, to accept and to live by your directions. Forgive us where we have failed, convince us where we still have doubts, empower us where we are weak, and give us hope where we doubt that making a change is even possible. Let this season bring us into a new place of surrender, trust, and reliance on your Holy Spirit. In Jesus name, amen.

———— ∞ ————

Questions for Reflection

❋ Do you accept the scriptures in today's devotion as teaching that Christians should abstain from sexual intimacy until after they are married? If so, are you willing to commit to wait (or cease if you've started) until your wedding day?

❋ What sexual guilt might you be carrying into your wedding day? Is there a mature believer, pastor, or counselor you can speak with to help you experience confession, repentance, and forgiveness? Do the two of you need to forgive each other so that you can enter marriage with a clean slate?

❋ What safeguards need to be put in place to help you stay true to your commitment until the wedding? What positive things can the two of you do during times when you used to be most vulnerable to sexual activity?

27

WONDROUS MARRIAGE

⚬⚬⚬

"... for better ..."

The weekend that Hurricane Harvey slammed into Houston, Lisa and I invited a married couple over to watch a sporting event. The rains hit hard just before the event started, so our neighborhood was transformed from asphalt streets to a flowing river between the time they arrived and the time they left.

Actually, the husband left a little earlier to check on their dog. The dog is old, deaf, and almost blind, but the wife was worried that she'd be scared, so she asked the husband to go get her (they live about a mile and a half away). He knew their feeble dog would hardly know it if a hurricane blew their house apart, but he loves his wife, so he went to their house. Because of road closures and the rain, it took him more than twenty minutes to make the drive one way and just as long to make it back.

His wife knew she was making a bit of an unreasonable request, but he went anyway. And while he was gone, she praised him as "one of the best husbands in the world."

You've probably heard many horror stories about what some married people have to put up with. Maybe some friends have even asked you why you'd want to get married in the first place, since so few marriages seem to be happy.

Don't believe them. We've met plenty of spouses, like our friend, who brag about their husbands or wives.

Numerous studies have shown that couples tend to be much happier than you might think. In fact, in her book *The Good News About Marriage*, Shaunti Feldhahn offers research that finds that about 80 percent of marriages are happy.

Which means you have a very good shot at a "for better" marriage.

When two people love God and each other, marriage can feel wonderful. And the even better news is that you can actually choose to have a "for better" marriage. You can both seek to spoil each other with kindness. You can be quick to forgive. You can display godly patience and great compassion for each other's struggles and even failures. And when you do—when your marriage is marked by the grace of Jesus Christ—you really can have a marriage described as "for better."

The pathway to a "for better" marriage is found in Colossians 3:12–14:

> Therefore, as God's chosen people, holy and dearly loved, clothe yourselves with compassion, kindness, humility, gentleness and patience. Bear with each other and forgive one another if any of you has a grievance against someone. Forgive as the Lord forgave you. And over all these virtues put on love, which binds them all together in perfect unity.

If you seek to put these into practice—display compassion for each other, look for ways to be kind to each other, be humble (put your spouse's needs above your own), be gentle and patient with each other, be quick to forgive, and seek to grow in loving each other—you will have a rich, intimate relationship that others will envy.

> You can actually choose to have a "for better" marriage.

There is truly no reason to be afraid as your wedding day gets ever nearer. With God's power within you, God's Word to guide you, and your resolve to apply Colossians 3:12–14 to your relationship, you can be confident that an intimate, satisfying marriage is yours to claim.

Heavenly Father, we accept this future marriage as a gift. Because of you, we can have great confidence that we are entering into a joyous phase of life. Release your peace and celebration into our hearts so we can truly enjoy the special day ahead when we pledge to become husband and wife. In Jesus' name, amen.

Questions for Reflection

※ What are some of your favorite "for better" moments with each other so far?

※ What do you most look forward to about being married to each other?

※ Go over the list of character qualities and actions in Colossians 3:12–14. What quality do you display most often? Is there an area in which you need to grow? Pray that God will help both of you fully live up to the high call of that great passage of Scripture.

28

MORE THAN CONQUERORS

"... for worse ..."

S tanding on the precipice of a new marriage, you have no idea how many or what kind of challenges you may face in the coming years and decades.

But I assure you, *there will be challenges.*

You are about to marry a man or woman who, as we've already mentioned, has a fragile body that can grow sick or become disabled.

You may not find out about your partner's deep psychological wounds, many of which won't manifest themselves until a little later in life, perhaps the early thirties, when a person finds out just how much damage was done to his or her psyche in the early years of life.

You may be treated unfairly by those outside your marriage, be cheated out of your lifelong savings; get fired from a job due to no fault of your own; suffer the consequences of someone else's mismanagement.

You may feel the sting of childlessness, or endure the pain of children who rebel.

You may face moral struggles, or find yourself married to a fellow believer who becomes besieged with doubts.

When you vow to be with your spouse until death takes you away, you don't know, you can't know, all that you are signing up for. That's what vows are all about. Life is not easy in a fallen world, but you are agreeing that the two of you will walk through this fallen world *together*. You will not let it tear you apart. You will not abandon each other during the dark moments. You will cling to each other, hand in hand, side by side, and keep moving toward each other, especially when this world seems particularly designed to pull you apart.

In Romans 8:37, the apostle Paul declared that "in all these things we are more than conquerors through him who loved us."

The shocking part of this verse is that it assumes life is best imaged by *combat*. Spiritual, social, and personal forces are moving to tear you apart as a couple. To not be engaged in the warfare, to pretend your relationship and your mission and your integrity aren't under

attack, is tantamount to having a picnic in the middle of a battlefield, and then being surprised when a grenade explodes under your table.

So, the passage in question calls us to admit the challenge (there's no conquering unless you're in the middle of warfare), but also to adopt higher expectations of what God can and will do. It won't be easy, but it is also more of a glorious conclusion than we could have imagined. Not only will you conquer, but you can become *more* than conquerors. Not only are you saved, but you can bring many others with you. Why not view each day of marriage as a moment for the two of you to conquer, a challenge to overcome, a battle to win together?

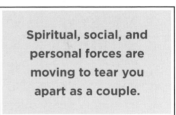

Spiritual, social, and personal forces are moving to tear you apart as a couple.

The reason Romans 8:37 is so important is that a defeatist attitude kills almost as many marriages as do affairs. "It's hopeless" becomes self-fulfilling.

Promising to be there during the "for worse" is motivating.

"We've already tried, and it didn't work" has set many weak marriages in the cement of disappointment.

Promising to stick together during the "for worse" helps you double down on hope.

Don't settle for less than being more than a conqueror. God wants more of you than to merely hold on and stay together. He would have you learn the lessons you must learn, conquer division in your home, and then become a couple advocate for other couples who are drowning in defeat, starving for joy, thirsting for oneness.

What will sustain you? Not your own wisdom, and certainly not your own power or goodness. We are more than conquerors, Paul told us, "through him who loved us." When we truly experience,

understand, rest in, and relish the love that is poured out on us—a knowledge and understanding dependent on divine revelation (Eph. 3:14–18)—we can live recklessly courageous marriages because we know God loves us, has our backs, and will lift us up. He can't be defeated.

Scripture calls us to rise up and say, "This day, together, in his name, we conquer!"

This might sound hopelessly hokey to some of you, but for others, it really could be a powerful start-the-day battle cry. We know that wars can be long, that battles sometimes involve momentary setbacks, but we take each day as a new opportunity to conquer, to gain new ground, to faithfully advance his kingdom. "Yesterday we might have had our teeth kicked in, but this day, in his name, together we conquer!"

―――――― ∞ ――――――

Heavenly Father, we don't know the challenges we will face, but you do. Prepare our hearts and minds. Help us grow more deeply in love with you and with each other so that when the battle rages, it will only bring us closer together as we seek to be more than conquerors, in your name and for your glory. Amen.

―――――― ∞ ――――――

Questions for Reflection

❋ What are some of the "for worse" moments you've faced so far in your relationship? What did you learn from them, both positive and negative?

❋ Describe a possible scenario in which the two of you could be seen as "more than conquerors." How do you need to grow—individually and in your relationship—for that to happen?

❋ Take each other's hands and entwine your fingers. Remind yourself that this is what you're promising to do, for the rest of your life. No matter how difficult it gets, no matter how frustrating it might be, you will take this person's hands into yours. You will hold on to them. You won't let them go. These are the hands you are promising to cling to for the rest of your days, for better *and for worse*.

29

MONEY, MONEY, MONEY

"For richer, for poorer . . ."

Did you know that Jesus talked about money more than he talked about heaven and hell *combined*? Close to eight hundred scriptures discuss money. About one-fourth of Jesus' parables are about money, and one out of every seven verses in the gospel of Luke discusses money.

Here's the real shocker, one that people can hardly believe: Jesus actually talked about money more than he talked about love.

Why do you think this might be true?

Money carries a spiritual weight that can lift you up or hold you down. It will bless you as a couple or it can become a deep divide.

Every one of us has a unique relationship with money that rarely gets discussed and that usually remains unconscious. Our feelings about money are visceral, deep-seated in the core of our being, and

many of us don't even recognize the way these feelings motivate us. Some of us deeply fear losing our money, and we react with panic and anger if it is threatened. Others of us are driven by greed to always have a little bit more, and we will sacrifice some of our most inti-mate relationships to make more time and energy available to procure more money. I have seen some literally sacrifice their health and peace of mind to bring "just a little bit more" into what already looks like an abundant pile of resources. For still others of us, we're driven by a simple selfishness that insists, "What's mine is mine" and are robbed of the tremendous joy found in giving. A few blessed souls have found that generosity with money brings great freedom.

The Bible does speak favorably of sensible saving (Genesis 41; Proverbs 21:20; Eccl. 11:2) but even more about generous giving (Deuteronomy 15:10; Psalm 112:5; Proverbs 22:9; Malachi 3:10; 2 Corinthians 9:6–10). It seems to suggest that financial planning is a wise thing to do (Proverbs 27:23–27) and exalts hard work over laziness (Proverbs 24:33–34; 2 Thessalonians 3:10). It also suggests that wanting to leave an inheritance behind is a good thing (Proverbs 13:22; 1 Timothy 5:8). All these together suggest that managing your money in a God-honoring way will bless you and nurture your marriage, while ignoring scriptural truths about handling money may bring much misery, frustration, and pain into your life and marriage. *Not* thinking about the best ways to manage your money will likely lead you to the default position of mishandling your money.

You and your future spouse will be combining your financial assets, so to become one, you're going to have to talk about your relationship with money. Even if you keep your money separate (though I hope you don't), how you save and spend your money will impact each other. Take an honest look into your own soul to discover just how you feel about money, in a way you may never have thought about it before.

What gives you the most joy? A certain level of savings? Knowing that you've given away a certain amount? Seeing others smile when you meet a need? Getting to buy something you've wanted for a very long time?

> As a Christian couple, *you need to give*, generously and often.

What gives you the most security? A certain credit score and a consistently growing retirement account? A secure job? Knowledge that your heavenly Father has promised to provide all your needs?

When working with premarital couples, I usually find that their giving is rather haphazard. They often give primarily on the spur of the moment, without a plan, when someone presents a dramatic need. If they had a close relative die of cancer, it is likely that they give a yearly donation to a cancer foundation of some kind. Others will say they take advantage of a charity their employer will match. Still others like to simply claim that they "tithe" with their time, and therefore don't really worry about how much money they give away.

As a Christian couple, *you need to give*, generously and often.

Sometimes, it should hurt. At the end of the year, when you add up all that you gave for tax purposes, it's okay to lose your breath for a second and think, *But we could have bought x, y, or z with that,* and then remind yourself, *Yet giving it to God's work was the best thing we could have done.*

Where you give your money reflects your heart. It's understandable that you would want to contribute to research to stop the spread of a disease that has afflicted a loved one; it's a good thing to want to support a local symphony or library. Yet Christians are told to seek *first* (primarily, above all other good things) "the kingdom of God" (Matthew 6:33 ESV). We should be all about living for and celebrating the spread of Christ's kingdom. That's why my wife and I like to focus on works that glorify Jesus and spread his Word. That doesn't mean we don't ever give to civic charities or medical pursuits. We do and we have. But it does mean that we want to invest most of what we give to work  where God is the hero, and where God is specifically exalted.

If you've never studied this issue, consider listening to Andy Stanley's three-part sermon series entitled "Crazy Like Us" (http://northpoint.org/messages/crazy-like-us/).

The reason I call evaluating your relationship with money "spiritual preparation" is that if you learn the lessons Andy talks about (there are three sermons; they would make for three great date-night discussions), money will be a positive force for good in your marriage rather than something that rips you apart.

The spiritual secret is this: generosity blesses the generous even more than it blesses those the generous people give to.

Since money troubles are a major factor in marital breakups, it's a wise investment at this stage of your relationship for you and your future spouse to spend a few hours examining your hearts and the Scriptures, and making a plan to be wise stewards of the resources God brings your way. Let your upcoming wedding be the launching pad for a new relationship with money.

If money was important enough for Jesus to talk about so much, it should be important enough for you to search out his teachings on the subject and discover just why he emphasized our relationship with money.

———— ∞ ————

Heavenly Father, let our upcoming union call us to a thoughtful awareness of our relationship with money. Help us understand our fears and motivations and beliefs about money, and give us hearts that honor you and your truth when it comes to how we should handle, save, and give our money. In Jesus' name, amen.

———— ∞ ————

Questions for Reflection

❋ Spend some time talking with each other about the way money motivates you. Maybe you've never even thought about it. Maybe it drives you to some unhealthy places. In the process of a prayerful conversation with God, ask the Lord to help you draw out each other's true motivations and heart issues when it comes to money.

❋ How can the two of you be more thoughtful about your relationship with money? Will you commit to watch Andy Stanley's sermon series? Would you prefer to go through a Christian-based financial program, such as Dave Ramsey's Financial Peace University? You might also benefit from reading through Randy Alcorn's *Money, Possessions, and Eternity* (Carol Stream, IL: Tyndale, 2003).

❋ Discuss how you can set some financial goals within the first year of marriage—after you've studied this a little more. Maybe you'll set a certain level of savings, decide on a certain amount or percentage that you hope to give away, or make a plan for getting out of debt. Resolve as a couple to take charge of and manage your money instead of letting it pull the two of you apart.

30

HUNGRY AGAIN

∞∞∞

". . . so long as you both shall live."

After a hard workout at the gym one evening, I came home to a wonderful meal prepared by my wife. It was a little late for dinner, about eight fifteen, and the challenging workout had only increased my hunger.

The meal was wonderful, just what I needed.

I woke up the next morning and after working for a while, wanted to go for another run. It was a bit frustrating, though, as I was . . . hungry.

Why?

I'd had a perfectly decent meal last night. Why should I be hungry again?

Could it be that though I'd had a good meal eleven hours ago, that doesn't mean I'd never be hungry again?

You've gone through a devotional to spiritually prepare yourself for marriage. You may also be taking the wise step of going through premarital counseling, where you're talking about major issues in your relationship. It should be no surprise that this is making you both feel a little closer to each other. You're "feeding" the relationship, so it's growing.

But the relationship will never reach a point where it doesn't need to be fed, any more than you could enjoy a two-hundred-dollar dinner and be satisfied for a full week. If you stop feeding your marriage, one or both of you will become hungry again.

The Bible stresses the need to persevere in doing the right thing: "Let us not become weary in doing good, for at the proper time we will reap a harvest if we do not give up" (Galatians 6:9).

The "harvest" results from *continuing* to do the right thing, working until the very end. You're not just choosing to *get* married; you're choosing to *be* married. That means feeding your marriage every day, "so long as you both shall live." You're promising not just to live together, but to grow toward each other. Your spouse

will have a legitimate expectation that, after the ceremony, you will make your relationship a top priority in your life. On your wedding day, you're not just saying, "I do." You're committing to, "I *will*. For the rest of my life."

I don't want this to sound like an obligation, but rather an invitation. It's not always comfortable to choose to work out, but the reason I do work out is because I feel better the other twenty-three hours of the day. I have more energy, less stress, more joy.

In the same way, when you feed your marriage, it's like pouring a river of contentment through your soul. Frustrations at work won't matter as much; agitations in other relationships won't sting so sharply; physical ills will

> On your wedding day, you're not just saying, "I do." You're committing to, "I *will*. For the rest of my life."

be easier to endure. A happy, well-connected marriage makes all of life more pleasant. The highs become more fun, and the lows feel less suffocating.

You won't always feel like "working" on your marriage, but it will always pay off (eventually) when you do. Investing in your marriage, in your intimacy, in your connectedness, will give you far more than it will cost you. Think of it this way: You're committing to have a lifetime of laughter! Passionate lovemaking! Soulful discussions! Too many meals together to count! Listening to each other's dreams! Perhaps raising children together!

You no longer have to wonder, *Will I find someone to love me?* or *What would it be like to be married to that person?* You get to live in reality. You get to take all the energy you spent wondering, *What if?* and now spend it living *what is*. For the rest of your life, your priorities become much simpler: God first. Your spouse second. Everything else fights for number three.

The search is over. A new life—a life of intimacy, joy, challenge, and purpose—begins.

Some of the most powerful, life-giving, exciting words you will ever agree to are, "so long as you both shall live."

Heavenly Father, there are so many good things to pursue in this wonderful world you have made, but guard my heart so that I don't put anything ahead of my relationship with you and then my relationship with my future spouse. Give me the commitment to feed my marriage on a daily basis. Don't let me become weary; don't let me become apathetic. I realize I am entering a relationship that will need to be nurtured for the rest of my life. In Jesus' name, amen.

Questions for Reflection

✳ List two or three things that you believe have most fed your relationship up to this moment. Will you commit to doing those same things in the future?

✳ What new things will marriage allow you to do to keep feeding your relationship that you haven't been able to do at this point in your journey?

✳ Discuss how taking the time to feed and care for your relationship will ultimately lead to more happiness; it may sound like work, but talk about how, in the end, it's work that will more than pay for itself.

A WEDDING DAY
MEDITATION FOR HER

⚬⚬⚬

From the time you were a little girl, God knew this day would make up a very special part of your life. He has anticipated, with great joy and celebration, the beginning of a brand-new family and the fashioning of one new person out of two.

This is a holy, joy-filled day!

You've no doubt spent months looking for just the right dress, the right earrings, the right shoes; you want this day to be special, and you want to look your absolute best. You want your soon-to-be husband to gasp when he sees you in all your beauty and glory, walking up the aisle to become his wife.

That's as it should be. But there's something else to remember on this very special day.

The Old Testament prophet Jeremiah was speaking for God when he asked, "Can a virgin forget her ornaments, or a bride her attire? Yet my people have forgotten me" (Jeremiah 2:32 ESV).

It's unimaginable that a bride would forget her dress before she walked up the aisle on her wedding day. Your dress is a central part of getting ready. It's inconceivable that you'd forget to put it on before walking up the aisle.

Jeremiah was saying that just as it's ludicrous to suggest a bride would forget to get dressed on her wedding day, it's equally ludicrous to imagine God's people forgetting he is with them. It should be that unthinkable to live even a moment without consciously remembering God.

If you're reading this on your wedding day (as I hope you are), then good for you for wanting to be spiritually prepared rather than just physically dressed on this milestone of a day. As you put on the beautiful dress and the jewelry, adorn yourself also with the spiritual ornaments of humility, reverence for God, and the remembrance of God.

Clothe yourself with humility as you prepare to walk down that aisle. You are a beloved daughter of God, but allow yourself to be a little humbled that a man has chosen you above all the other women in the world, and is about to give his full life to you—not because you're not worthy, but because it is still such an awesome gift and commitment. Be grateful that God has given you a husband to stand by you, a man with whom you can raise children, a partner with whom you can laugh and sometimes cry.

Recognize, with humility, that you don't have what it takes within you to fulfill the vows you are about to make. You cannot love unconditionally, as the Bible calls you to love, without the Holy Spirit. Worship until you get to the point that you can actually say, and truly believe, "God, I need your Spirit more than I need this dress to walk down this aisle and to make such an awesome commitment."

This day is an act of worship and a new call to a new dependence on God and a new awareness of his provision. According to Jeremiah, God said, "Before I formed you in the womb I knew you, and before you were born I consecrated you" (1:5). God thought up the essence of who you are, what you would look like, your personality, your skills at being a ruling regent of the earth (Genesis 1:28), a wife (Genesis 2:18), and a mom (Genesis 1:28), and he knew from your first day who you would fall in love with and choose to marry. Everything about this day is because of him, so don't forget him. Let his name be on your lips; let his praise fill your heart; let his Spirit give you the courage to say the vows you are about to say.

As you see your soon-to-be husband standing in front of the church, waiting for you, make the walk worshipful and prayerful. Thank God for the gift you are about to receive. Implore God to make you worthy and faithful to the promises you are about to give. This will be one of the most fascinating and significant moments of your life—invite God to fill every minute of it.

Better to forget your wedding dress and to walk down the aisle in a borrowed pair of sweat pants than to forget your God on this most special of days. Make him the center of your thoughts with every step you take as you walk into a brand-new life, together with your future husband.

A WEDDING DAY
MEDITATION FOR HIM

⁓

Y ou are about to experience one of the most memorable moments of a man's life: watching your beautiful bride walk up the aisle to become your wife. I pray that God would allow time to stand still for you so you will remember this moment and fully embrace this once-in-a-lifetime experience.

As you let your eyes feast on the sight of your wife, let your thoughts also leave room for the kind, generous, and loving God who has made this day possible. When you were yet a young boy, God looked forward to the day when, as a man, you would choose this woman with whom you will spend your life. He shares in your joy and happiness, and he wants you to experience marriage to the fullest and to receive this joyful day as a gift from him.

What he doesn't want is to be cast aside as an afterthought, forgotten, as if he doesn't exist. In a sobering passage spoken through the Old Testament prophet Jeremiah, God challenges his people, "Can a virgin forget her ornaments, or a bride her attire? Yet my people have forgotten me" (Jeremiah 2:32 esv).

Some couples choose to have spur-of-the-moment or very casual weddings, but most of the time the bride has thought long and hard about what she will wear on this important day. Can you even imagine your future wife waking up today and saying to herself, *Huh. I wonder what I should wear to my wedding . . . ?*

Just as absurd as that, Jeremiah told us, is God's people forgetting him. It should be unthinkable!

And while Jeremiah was addressing the bride, he could just as well have said, "Groom, better that you should stand in front of the church in your boxer briefs than you should watch your bride come down the aisle forgetting that God created that supremely beautiful woman who is about to join her hand with yours."

Her smile? God's idea.

Her laugh? God tuned that, just perfectly.

The softness of her skin, the intoxication of her mystery—yeah, he thought all that up too. Would that every groom would pray, enamored with the glory of the woman walking down the aisle, "Lord, you've blessed me in more ways than I could count; you've given me so many rich and wonderful things, but this surpasses them all!"

If you're not worshipping during your wedding ceremony, you're not paying attention.

Begin the ceremony with an appropriate humility. I'm sure you're a great guy. After all, you had the great sense to read this book, and you're even following through reading it on your wedding day! But as great as you may be, no one really "deserves" the commitment of marriage. Another person is committing to be with you, to stay true to you, to face all that life offers, to give her hopes, her dreams, her body, and her time to you until one of you should die. That's a stunning commitment.

Why am I so insistent on making God a big part of this celebration? As a guy who has sought to be true to his vows for more than thirty years, let me tell you that you're going to need God to love this woman as God calls you to love her. We men can't love like Christ without Christ. You will need God to be an active agent in your life perhaps more than you've ever needed him before.

Mentally pause before this day rushes by. Imagine God himself, with his hands on your shoulders, whispering to you, "You can do this, son, because there won't be a minute of marriage, not even a second, when I won't be loving her through you. Stay near to me, listen to me, and I will show you what a truly abundant life there can be in the center of a holy, sanctified, and sacred marriage."

As you put on your tux, let this truth wash over you: be thankful, humble, worshipful, hopeful, and grateful, because it's going to be one of the most momentous days of your life.

NOTES

⸺⸺⸺∞⸺⸺⸺

Chapter 1: Celebrating the Joys of Marriage

1. Gary Thomas, *Sacred Marriage*, rev. ed. (Grand Rapids: Zondervan, 2015), 13.

Chapter 2: God's Invention

1. Martin Luther, "The Estate of Marriage," *Luther's Works*, vol. 45, ed. Walther L. Brandt (Minneapolis: Fortress, 1962), reprinted in Dana Mack and David Blankenhorn, eds., *The Book of Marriage: The Wisest Answers to the Toughest Questions* (Grand Rapids: Eerdmans, 2001), 368–69.
2. Luther, in Mack and Blankenhorn, 371.

Chapter 3: You're Going on a Journey

1. C. S. Lewis, *Letters to Malcolm, Chiefly on Prayer* (New York: Mariner Books, 2016), 76.

Chapter 13: Don't Believe the Lies

1. William Gurnall, *The Christian in Complete Armour: A Treatise of the Saints' War Against the Devil,* vol. 1 (London: Blackie and Son, 1865), 94, paraphrased.

Chapter 15: The Guilt of "Tempting Another Soul"

1. Clarence Macartney, *Sermons from Life* (Nashville: Cokesbury Press, 1933),155.

Chapter 21: The Highest Place

1. John Wesley, "The Duties of Husbands and Wives" (sermon), cited in Doreen Moore, *Good Christians, Good Husbands? Leaving a Legacy in Marriage and Ministry* (Roo-shire, UK: Christian Focus Publications, 2004), 24–25.

Chapter 22: Broken Bodies

1. This and subsequent letters shared in this devotional are cited in "The Love of Charles and Susannah Spurgeon," Church History Timeline, on Christianity.com, http://www.christianity.com/church/church-history/timeline/2001-now/the-love-of-charles-and-susannah-spurgeon-11633045.html.
2. Cited in "The Love of Charles and Susannah Spurgeon," Church History Timeline, on Christianity.com: http://www.christianity.com/church/church-history/timeline/2001-now/the-love-of-charles-and-susannah-spurgeon-11633045.html

ACKNOWLEDGMENTS

I'd like to thank those who read and commented on earlier versions of this manuscript: Alli Sepulveda, T. W. S. Hunt, Mary Kay Smith, Andrea Perkins, Kelsey Thomas, and Lisa Thomas.

From Zondervan, thanks go out to David Morris (every writer should be so blessed to have such a publisher as David), Kristen Parrish, Renee Chavez, Michael Aulisio, Tim Marshall, Mandy Wilson, and Hannah Cannon.

I thank God daily for the wonderful group of people known as Second Baptist Church in Houston, Texas. Their support and partnership in this ministry have been one of the great joys of my life.

A final shout-out to my agents, Mike Salisbury and Curtis Yates, who both are true friends, fellow servants, and brothers in the Lord.

ABOUT GARY THOMAS

⬡

G ary Thomas is a writer-in-residence who also serves on the teaching team at Second Baptist Church in Houston, Texas, and the author of eighteen books, including the bestselling *Sacred Marriage*, that have sold more than a million copies worldwide and have been translated into a dozen languages. He and his wife, Lisa, have been married for thirty-three years.

You can connect with Gary via his blog: www.garythomas.com/blog
Twitter: @garyLthomas
Facebook: www.facebook.com/authorgarythomas

For information about Gary's ministry and his speaking schedule, visit his website at www.garythomas.com. To inquire about inviting Gary to your church, please email Alli@garythomas.com, or make a request through the website.